Seven-Card Stud
for Advanced Players
21st Century Edition

By

David Sklansky, Mason Malmuth, and Ray Zee

A product of Two Plus Two Publishing

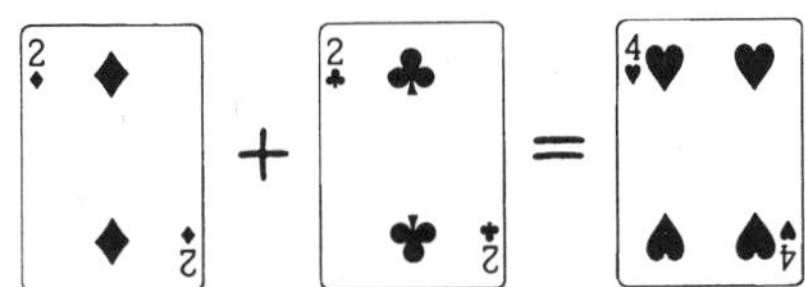

FOURTH EDITION
FIRST PRINTING: June 1999

Printing and Binding
Creel Printing & Publishing Co.
Las Vegas, Nevada

Printed in the United States of America

Seven-Card Stud for Advanced Players

For information address:

Two Plus Two Publishing.
226 Garfield Dr.
Henderson, NV 89014
702-896-1326

ISBN: 1-880685-23-X

To Jackie Stark

Table of Contents

About David Sklansky

David Sklansky is generally considered the number one authority on gambling in the world today. Besides his nine books on the subject, David also has produced two videos and numerous writings for various gaming publications. His occasional poker seminars always receive an enthusiastic reception including those given at the Taj Mahal in Atlantic City and the World Series of Poker in Las Vegas.

More recently David has been doing consulting work for casinos, Internet gaming sites, and gaming device companies. He has recently invented a new game called *Poker Challenge,* soon to appear in casinos.

David attributes his standing in the gambling community to three things:

1. The fact that he presents his ideas as simply as possible (sometimes with Mason Malmuth) even though these ideas frequently involve concepts that are deep, subtle, and not to be found elsewhere.
2. The fact that the things he says and writes can be counted on to be accurate.
3. The fact that to this day a large portion of his income is still derived from gambling (usually poker but occasionally blackjack, sports betting, horses, video games, casino promotions, or casino tournaments).

Thus, those who depend on David's advice know that he still depends on it himself.

Other Books by David Sklansky

Hold 'em Poker
The Theory of Poker
Getting The Best of It

Sklansky on Poker
Poker, Gaming, and Life
Sklansky Talks Blackjack

Gambling for a Living by David Sklansky and Mason Malmuth
Hold 'em Poker for Advanced Players by David Sklansky and Mason Malmuth

About Mason Malmuth

Mason Malmuth was born and raised in Coral Gables, Florida. In 1973 he received his BS in Mathematics from Virginia Tech, and completed their Masters' program in 1975. While working for the United States Census Bureau in 1978, Mason stopped overnight in Las Vegas while driving to his new assignment in California. He was immediately fascinated by the games, and gambling became his major interest.

After arriving in California he discovered that poker was legal and began playing in some of the public cardrooms as well as taking periodic trips to Las Vegas where he would play both poker and blackjack. In 1981 he went to work for the Northrop Corporation as a mathematician and moved to Los Angeles where he could conviently pursue his interest in poker in the large public cardrooms in Gardena, Bell Gardens, and Commerce.

In 1983 his first article "Card Domination — The Ultimate Blackjack Weapon" was published in *Gambling Times* magazine. In 1987 he left his job with the Northrop Corporation to begin a career as both a full-time gambler and a gambling writer. He has had over 500 articles published in various magazines and is the author or co-author of 12 books. These include *Gambling Theory and Other Topics,* where he tries to demonstrate why only a small number of people are highly successful at gambling. In this book he introduces the reader to the concept of "non-self weighting strategies" and explains why successful gambling is actually a balance of luck and skill. Other books he has co-authored are *Hold 'em Poker For Advanced Players,* written with David Sklansky, and *Seven-Card Stud for Advanced Players* written with David Sklansky and Ray Zee. All the "advanced" books are considered the definitive works on these games.

His company Two Plus Two Publishing has sold over 300,000 books and currently has 22 titles to its credit. These books are recognized as the best in their field and are thoroughly studied by those individuals who take gambling seriously.

Other Books by Mason Malmth

Gambling Theory and Other Topics
Poker Essays
Poker Essays, Volume II
Blackjack Essays
Winning Concepts in Draw and Lowball

Gambling for a Living by David Sklansky and Mason Malmuth
Hold 'em Poker for Advanced Players by David Sklansky and Mason Malmuth

Booklets with Mason Malmuth

Fundamentals of Craps by Mason Malmuth and Lynne Loomis
Fundamentals of Poker by Mason Malmuth and Lynne Loomis
Fundamentals of "21" by Mason Malmuth and Lynne Loomis
Fundamentals of Video Poker by Mason Malmuth and Lynne Loomis

About Ray Zee

Ray Zee was born and raised in New Jersey, and spent his college years in the East as well. Unlike other students, Ray did more than just study. He began to gamble on the side in school, and when he graduated he was ready to start his career, which just happened to be in the dessert of Nevada.

Ray quickly realized that there were many opportunities in various forms of gambling and began to search for ways to exploit the inequities in many of the games. This included blackjack, horse racing, sports betting, slot jackpots, and of course his favorite game, poker.

It wasn't long before he became known as one of the top poker players and most knowledgeable gamblers in the world. And when we say world, we mean it literally because there are very few places where gambling is offered that Ray has not visited. In fact, you can go to many cardrooms all over the world, mention the name Ray Zee, and get an immediate response.

Ray usually chooses to play in very high stakes cash games, many of which feature some of the best players in the world. It has been said that "He leaves them with their eyes wide open when he departs." Ray is also one of the very few players that is considered expert in virtually every form of poker played for serious money. He is also one of the very few gamblers (still around) that has been to all the World Series of Poker Tournaments at Binnions Horseshoe Hotel and Casino in Las Vegas.

Rays book, *High-Low-Split Poker for Advanced Players* is recognized as the premier book on split pot games, and this has increased his following and helped to promote these games as well. He is considered an invaluable member of the Two Plus Two Publishing team, and his advice and wisdom is widely sought by many of his peers and adversaries at the gaming tables.

Introduction

Seven-card stud is an extremely complicated game. How complicated is it? Well, it is so complicated that it is probably impossible for any book written on the subject to be truly complete. This is simply because there is an almost infinite number of unique situations that can occur, each requiring separate analysis. Consequently, even though you are about to read solid guidelines to winning, the strategies given are not set in concrete, and under certain conditions, the best strategies occasionally may differ slightly from what is recommended.

This being noted, rest assured that what follows is a very strong winning approach. If it weren't, we would not be in a position to write this book simply because we would be broke and standing on the rail.

In the past, little information has been available on seven-card stud. Even though the game is widely played, few authors have attempted to attack it. This is probably for the best, because the large amount of erroneous and silly information/advice that seems to dominate poker literature has not infiltrated seven-card stud.

This book basically teaches a tight but aggressive approach. However, we will be recommending that you play more hands than you might have expected (though we will tell you to throw away some surprising hands as well). This is partly because we are addressing advanced players. If you are new to stud, even if you are experienced at another form of poker, you probably will want to play somewhat tighter and more conservatively than what the text indicates. However, with experience, you can completely follow our guidelines to play seemingly loose at times.

All great seven-card stud players have a "feel" for the game. This comes only with serious study, thinking about the game, and extensive experience. In truth, becoming an expert seven-card stud player, even with the help of this book, will not be easy.

However, with a great deal of time and effort, it can certainly be accomplished.

Keep in mind that the strategies which follow are designed for the medium limit games, most specifically the $15-$30 limit with a $2 ante and a $5 low card bring-in, up through the $30-$60 limit with a $5 ante and $10 low card bring-in. But they will be valuable for many other limits as well. However, don't jump into a large limit game after a quick reading of this book. As one of the authors (Ray) likes to say, "You will get killed." At the higher limits, you will run into many expert players who easily can manipulate someone new to the game into making many costly mistakes. Conversely, in the smaller games, many of the sophisticated plays used to manipulate opponents into making errors do not work, as your opponents are not aware enough to be tricked. In spite of this, many of the ideas in this text will help you at the smaller games while you work your way up to the bigger ones. As for the bigger games where players are capable of thinking at many different levels, studying the information in this book — gaining a great deal of experience and doing some hard thinking about the game — is the only way to guarantee success.

The original version of this text was written in 1989. Since then, stud has grown in popularity, as all poker has, but not at the rate at which hold 'em has grown. However, for high limit players, it is still the game of choice. On the East Coast it is the most popular form of poker. Likewise, many good games exist in other locations throughout the country.

This twenty-first century edition has been substantially expanded. We did this for several reasons, but the most important reason for the change was to help aspiring stud players approach the game from a proper perspective. You see, stud is not only a difficult game to play at an expert level, it is also a difficult game to teach well. We felt that additional material was needed to make expert play accessible to more people.

We also wanted to address loose games at a much deeper level. Because of the poker explosion that has taken place throughout the country during the past decade, numerous new players are at the tables, and many of them have come to "gamble." Thus, many games have become much looser. You should find some of the advice that we give in this area to be surprising, but be assured that it is accurate, and that these are techniques that we use in our play.

We also want to point out that medium and high limit seven-card stud is accompanied by a great deal of short-term luck. The effect of this is that the bad player, who originally stays away from seven-card stud because the game appears too complicated, might become attracted to it since he discovers that he can win more often than in some of the other forms of poker. Thus stud games have the potential to be good for a very long time, and many veteran players literally give their money to the experts.

We also want to pause for a moment and thank those people who helped us put this 21st Century Edition together. These include Irving Sklansky for his dedicated editing; Charmaine Dadian for her help in production and proofreading; Dave Clint for his superb art work and cover design; and Lynne Loomis for her many contributions and original editing of the previous edition. Without their help, this text would not meet the high standards that we set out to achieve.

Using This Book

Reading this book is not enough. You will also need to do a lot of thinking. It is recommended that the entire text be read first, later returning to those sections that require more study.

Keep in mind that we wrote this book for advanced players. If you are new to seven-card stud, it is probably best to play a little more conservatively than we recommend. However, once you have gained some experience, you should begin to see where it is appropriate to add all the plays we discuss.

We do not recommend that you jump right into a $30-$60 or higher limit game. Even though the strategies in this book will do well at the higher limits, especially if the opposition is not too tough, it is still better to start small and work your way up. In a game as complex as seven-card stud, there is no substitute for experience, and this game probably requires more experience than any other poker game.

However, the information that this text provides is not always accurate at limits below $15-$30. This is because the ante is proportionately smaller at the lower limits which changes optimal strategy from that of frequently wanting to knock out other players, to instead trapping your opponent. There will be more discussion on this later in the text.

One nice aspect of seven-card stud is that when you think you have the best hand, it is usually correct to bet. However, understanding exactly what the best hand is can at times be difficult. A common mistake made by beginners is to play a hand that appears to be good but is not really worthwhile. In addition, the hand that ranks the highest on a particular street is not necessarily the truly best hand. Thus you should pay strict attention to when hands are playable and when they are not, and exactly how they should be played. Failure to do so is probably the most common error that the typical player makes at this form of poker.

Seven-Card Stud for Advanced Players was written using the standard $15-$30 limit game as a model. The standard structure is a $2 ante and a $5 bring-in. Bets and raises on third and fourth street are in $15 increments, while bets and raises on fifth, sixth, and seventh streets are in $30 increments. The only exception occurs when a pair shows on fourth street, which now allows for either a $15 or a $30 bet. Other limits, such as $20-$40 with a $3 ante and a $5 bring-in, and $30-$60 with a $5 ante and $10 bring-in are similar enough in most situations that you will have to make few adjustments to what we recommend. However, where appropriate, we will supply some hints in this area.

Note that cards designated in the text are either underlined or not. If a card is underlined, then it is a hole card; otherwise it is an upcard. For example, if you see A♣A♠A♥, then your hand is three aces, and the two black aces are down.

Finally, we would like to take a moment to recommend *The Theory of Poker* by David Sklansky. Many of the general concepts essential to beating seven-card stud are discussed in detail in that work. In fact, a full understanding of the more specific ideas in this book will be difficult to achieve without also reading *The Theory of Poker*.

Why Play Seven-Card Stud?

There is one overriding reason to play seven-card stud rather than other games. It is simply that stud games tend to be very good. Why is this so? It probably has something to do with the fact that most tourists are familiar with it, and are thus more likely to sit down at a stud table. Another reason is that the large short-term luck factor in this form of poker attracts the bad players, as they are able to make some pretty decent scores every now and then, even though they will go broke in the long run. Whatever the reason, seven-card stud games are consistently better than any other form of poker, particularly in the bigger games.[1] The real expert almost always can find a stud game where his winning expectation is quite high.

But the large short-term luck factor, caused mainly by the fact that it is easier to "draw out" on the best hand than it is in a game like hold 'em, needs to be addressed. Most seven-card stud professionals talk about the "roller coaster ride" that they often seem to be on. Specifically, the large standard deviation inherent in this game requires a fairly large bankroll to ensure survival. Exactly how large your bankroll should be is the subject of a major section in *Gambling Theory and Other Topics* by Mason Malmuth. (Suffice it to say that many professionals are probably playing stakes where their bankrolls are in jeopardy.)

Also, keep in mind that there are two main reasons why you win money at stud. The first is that some of your opponents play badly and, in extreme cases, literally give their money away. The second is that this form of poker provides numerous opportunities for the expert player to make expert plays and extract additional money from his weaker-playing opponents. We are not referring

---

[1] In areas where poker is new, the stud games may not be as good as the hold 'em games, especially at the middle limits and below, but they should still be pretty good.

to merely bluffs. Rather, these expert plays allow you to gain an extra bet here and there, or perhaps to save a bet. In addition, optimal strategy may "save" you the pot by occasionally knocking out the best hand, or the potentially best hand. The expert player does a much better job of evaluating the value of his hand than does the typical player. We shall see that many factors, besides the cards that you hold, determine how strong your hand really is.

Remember, seven-card stud can be a rewarding game, but it also can be very frustrating. Stud hasn't grown as fast as other forms of poker, notably Texas hold 'em. But at the time of this writing, there are many games available throughout the United States, and it is the most popular game on the East Coast and in many European countries. So what's the bottom line? It is that if you become an expert at this form of poker, you should do very well indeed. But you won't become a champion overnight. It will take lots of study and playing experience, and, as just mentioned, will be frustrating at times. In fact, it will take longer to master stud than virtually any other form of poker. But it is also more fun to play than most other poker games "spread" in casinos, so trying to master this game at an advanced level is a goal well worth striving for.

A Note on the English

Neither one of us claim to be professional writers. We are professional poker players. Furthermore, the ideas and concepts presented in this book originally came from tape-recorded conversations between the authors. These tape recordings were not necessarily formatted exactly the same way a book would be and the language was not always grammatically perfect. This is occasionally reflected in the wording of this text.

But the purpose of this book is not to get an "A" from our English teacher. Rather it is to show you how to make a lot of money in all but the toughest seven-card stud games. So if we end a sentence with a preposition or use a few too many words or even introduce a new subject in a slightly inappropriate place, you can take solace from the fact that you can buy lots more books by Hemingway with the money we make you.

Part One

Third Street

Third Street

Introduction

The most important decision that you will make playing seven-card stud is on third street. Not only must you address the obvious question of *whether* to play your hand, but you also must determine *how* to play your hand. Some hands, such as large pairs, do better against a small number of opponents; other hands, such as a small three-flush, do best against a large number of opponents. A number of hands, such as a three-flush with two high cards, play well no matter how many opponents you may have (but we will shortly see that they usually prefer a short-handed pot).

In this section we will be talking about how to play your starting hands, as well as explaining why many hands typically played by others are not profitable. We also will show that some hands, which most people throw away, can be played for profit in certain situations, especially when you understand the game and your judgement is good.

As you will see, correct strategy on your first three cards is fairly complicated. You not only must be aware of the other players' upcards, but also of how well your opponents play, how tight or loose the game is, and how easy your competitors, especially those already in the pot, are to control and manipulate.

These are advanced concepts. But this is a book for advanced players. Once again, if you are new to seven-card stud, we recommend that you play somewhat more conservatively than what we advise. However, as you become more experienced, you can begin to play in line with what we advocate.

The Cards That Are Out

There are two concepts that are important to stud that most people do not properly take into account. The first is adjusting to the cards that are out. (The second concept, the number of players in the pot, will be addressed in the next chapter.) Just about everyone who plays seven-card stud knows the other upcards have an impact on the way a hand should be played, particularly on third street. But this concept has even more importance (especially in an eight-handed game) than most people realize. For instance, in extreme cases, you should throw the "best" hand away.

Here's an example. Suppose you start with

 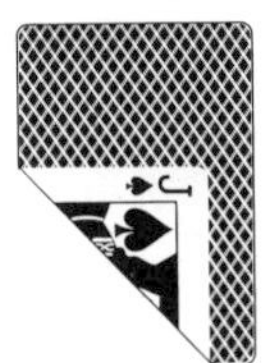 

and both jacks and a six are out. Further suppose that a deuce brings it in, a five raises, and then three other people call. Even though there is a good chance that you have the best hand on third street, you should throw the hand away. In fact, even if you somehow were 100 percent sure that you had the best hand, it still would be correct to fold. The reason for this is simply that seven-card stud, as its name implies, is a seven-card game. The only time that it would be correct to play this hand with those cards out is if it had a good chance to steal the antes, or possibly if you can get in cheaply in an unraised pot and one of the jacks is showing instead of the 6♥. Now you can call, trying to catch a scare card and hope to win the pot before the showdown. However, even this call is best against only one predictable opponent over whom you have good control.

On the other hand, weak hands that are completely live (in other words, none of your cards are gone), whether they are straight draws, pairs, or whatever, are usually worth playing. However, a small pair with a small, unrelated kicker still should usually be thrown away if the bring-in was raised to a full bet. (Pairs with high or related kickers will be discussed later in the text.)

A decent hand that is only partially dead may very well not be worth playing, and if it is almost completely dead, as in the example just given, it is almost certainly not worth playing, even if it is probably the best starting hand. (Two aces is normally an exception. Another possible exception is two kings, except against an ace showing.)

For example, suppose you start with:

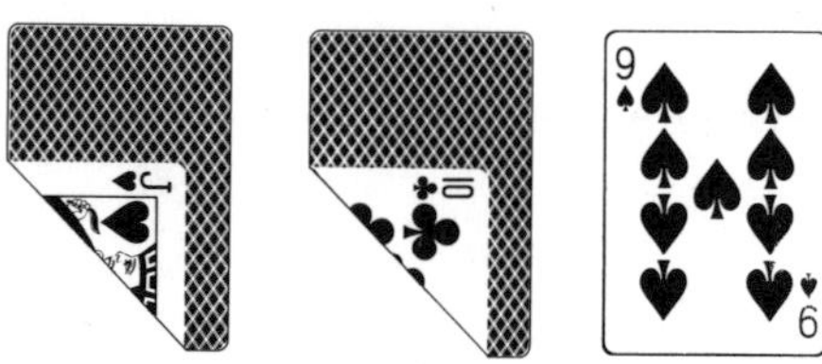

There is a big difference in the value of this hand if all the queens and eights are live, compared to if even just two of them are gone. In the first case you should always play it. In the second case you might not (especially if an ace, king, or queen raised).

Thus, you should be very aware of the cards that are out, especially on third street. Of course, you should not ignore the other cards that get turned up. However, since your starting decision is the most crucial, the initial upcards are the most crucial to remember.

It is important to understand that unless you are a real expert, getting out of line on third street can compound matters on the later streets. For example, if you play the pair of jacks mentioned earlier (remember your hand is very dead), you may get in deeper and deeper, with virtually no chance of winning. Only the great players can get out of these kinds of compounding problems. This is because they are able to maneuver weak opponents and obtain value out of their marginal hands. However, it takes an extremely long time to become good enough to get away with playing mediocre hands. And you can win plenty of money without ever reaching that point.

The Number of Players in the Pot

The second concept that most people do not properly take into account is realizing how certain hands change value depending on the number of players in the pot. Very few stud players fully understand this concept.

In hold 'em the value of a hand is less dependent upon the number of players in the pot. Furthermore, there aren't any upcards to take into account. Thus, hand values remain much more stable. This is why you can produce approximate hand rankings for hold 'em, but you can't for stud.

If you have a hand that prefers a small number of players rather than a lot of players, and you get a chance to knock people out, you should, of course, do it. However, if this is not possible, proper strategy now may be to play your hand much differently than if you were able to limit the field.

A hand that plays best by knocking people out doesn't have to be especially good or especially bad. It just has to have a particular characteristic to it. That is, it needs to do better short-handed than multiway.

For instance, suppose you have a hand that, when played heads-up will increase your chances of winning from 20 percent to 40 percent. Then you should make an effort to achieve this status. But the same would be true if getting heads-up would increase your chances of winning from 60 percent to 80 percent. Notice that we are talking about hands that may be totally different in relation to how good they are. Nonetheless, they both prefer to be heads-up, as they each will have a higher expectation if you can achieve this.

This is a concept that many inexperienced stud players have difficulty with. It seems counter-intuitive to put extra money in with a hand that clearly is not the best hand. Yet in those situations, where achieving a heads-up or short-handed pot is desirable, that additional bet needs to go in.

In many cases if you have a good hand that has much higher expectation heads-up and you can't get heads-up, you should now change your strategy. This usually means to call instead of raise because the hand will have lost much of its value. It can occur that you have a weak hand that you would rather play heads-up and if you can't achieve this, you should actually now fold.

This last idea is very important. To be a successful stud player you must understand that there are many hands that you will be dealt which are only playable as long as you are heads-up (or at least in a short-handed situation). When this cannot be achieved, these hands should be quickly discarded.

A simple example is a small pair with a pretty good kicker. Heads-up against a larger pair, which is smaller than your kicker, this hand is profitable. For example, you would want to play

heads-up against a probable pair of jacks. The reason for this is that you will frequently win when you improve to two pair. However, against many opponents two pair doesn't do very well.

In addition, there are some hands which don't appear to be good heads-up, but actually should be played that way, or at least they should be played in a way that thins down the field. This is true partially because it is better mathematically, and partially because it may help you get a free card. For instance, if you have the low card, three or four people limp, a high card raises, and you have an ace high three-flush, reraise almost every time — especially if your cards are live. We will see shortly that three-flushes normally prefer multiway pots. However, a live ace can make a difference. If you have two overcards over the raiser you should always reraise.

So why not call and just let everyone in? First of all, it's always possible that everyone may call anyway, which is okay. Second, it is very unlikely that you will get reraised on third street. For example, suppose you bring it in and your hand is:

Now a seven calls, a five calls, a four calls, a jack raises, and you reraise. Whether everyone folds or not, the jack is not going to raise again with just a pair of jacks.

Furthermore, on the next card the jack will assume that you have a big pair in the hole and will almost always check to you. You should usually bet no matter what you catch. On fifth street, assuming that you are still low, he will again almost always check, and you can take a free card. If, on the other hand, you caught anything good, you should bet again. (If you make a small open pair he might fold thinking that you have made two pair higher than jacks up.)

Notice that playing the hand this way will probably save you money in case you miss, and it increases the chance of winning if you catch an ace or make an open pair. This is an example of a hand that you should try to get heads-up with, even though it might at first appear to be a multiway hand.

Ante Stealing

First, let's define what we mean by "ante stealing." We mean trying to win the antes by raising with a hand that figures to be in trouble if it is called.

Understand that in most games you are getting pot odds of about 4-to-3 on your ante steal. This means that your steal has to work about 40 percent of the time to show an immediate profit. However, your chances actually don't need to be that good, because you may win later on. Only if your hand has absolutely no chance to win, except on the steal, would the 40 percent figure be correct.

Thus, it is usually worth a try to steal the antes, even if your chances for success are less than 40 percent, and particularly if the next card can win you the pot immediately. An example would be when you raise with an ace and catch an ace. This will happen about 6 percent of the time. In addition, catching this ace has allowed you to win an additional bet. You may also be able to win the pot on fourth street if you catch a card like a king suited to your ace.

There are other ways of being able to gain equity on the next card. Suppose it gives you a hand strong enough that it would be wrong for someone to call your bet on fourth street if he knew what your hole cards were. This is an important concept.

Here's an example. You raise with

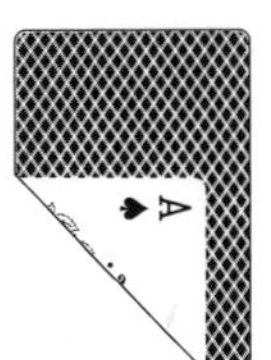

and a pair smaller than kings calls you. If you catch an ace or a king and your opponent knew that you had one of these cards in the hole, he should fold, providing that he does not improve. (See *The Theory of Poker* by David Sklansky for more discussion of this idea.) Notice that your chance of catching an ace or a king is about 12 percent. Plus you have another 6 percent chance of making open nines. So you have almost an 18 percent chance of winning the pot on fourth street if your opponent will fold small pairs if you catch an ace or a king or if you pair your door card, and you do even better if he doesn't fold against the ace or king.

Another idea to keep in mind is that when you catch a scare card, the type of hands that your opponents are likely to throw away are those hands made up of lower pairs than your board cards. Suppose that on fourth street, your board is:

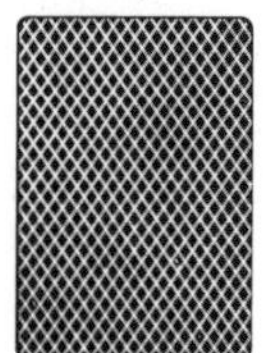

Your opponent is likely to throw away any hand up to two jacks. This means that when you are on a steal, also consider how high your opponents' upcards are.

So what's the bottom line? In general, raise with hands that have about a 30 percent chance of stealing if the game is at least moderately tight. This usually means having the highest card showing, with half-decent cards in the hole; or the second highest upcard, with fair cards in the hole. But as the game gets looser, your hand needs to be progressively better to try to steal even with the high card. And if you are inexperienced you should steal even less yet.

Of course, the best highest card to have showing is an ace. The reason having an ace up is especially good is that opponents, with the exception of being rolled up, never can have the hand that you are representing, beat. That is, you are safer as far as not getting reraised. If instead, for example, your jack was the highest card showing, someone may have a bigger pair in the hole.

If you don't have the highest upcard, you risk being reraised by the person who does. And if he is a good player, you may be reraised even if he does not have what he is representing. Therefore, be less apt to steal the antes without the highest card showing, especially if there is one or more aggressive or tough players showing higher cards yet to act.

However, the second highest upcard showing is frequently a better stealing hand than it appears. Suppose one of the remaining players holds a small pair. He may be quick to play against someone who raises with the highest upcard, especially if several players have passed, because he is unwilling to give that person credit for a hand. However, if you raise (as a steal) with a higher card still to act behind you, it will appear that your hand is real. You raised into a higher card, didn't you? Thus, if you get past the player with the highest card showing, you may also get someone with a small pair to throw their hand away. So if the high card is held by an unimaginative, predictable, or timid player, and you hold the second highest upcard, your hand may become a candidate for a steal.

On the other side of the coin, you should also be willing to *reraise* when you hold the highest upcard, but don't necessarily have the raiser beat. For example, suppose you are in a tough game, your opponent raises with a ten, and you have a queen up with a three-flush or any of the other playable hands that you should at least call with. Now you should sometimes reraise. Notice that if your opponent is "semi-bluffing," you often will win the pot immediately. (He might even fold two tens.) However, this play is correct only because you are holding a legitimate hand that has a good chance of beating your opponent.

What if you are in an early position? Is it correct to steal up front? The answer is, "occasionally," but only if the game is tight, and generally only when you have the highest card showing. Furthermore, you should usually limit your steal raises (in an early position) to those times when you have an ace or a king up. If the game is loose, trying to steal up front is usually a mistake. In these games you need a legitimate hand to raise when many players still remain to act behind you.

If the highest card is held by a player who folds a lot and doesn't reraise without a bigger pair than he possibly faces, you can raise as a steal with the second highest card from an early position. However, be sure that you are correct in your evaluation of that player.

Also, regardless of your position, do not make these raises at random. They should be based on the strength of your hand and on the other upcards. In addition, you can raise more when you are facing duplicate upcards.

Here's an example incorporating this last idea. Suppose your hand is:

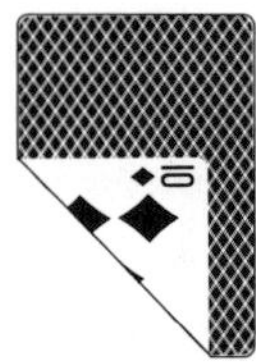
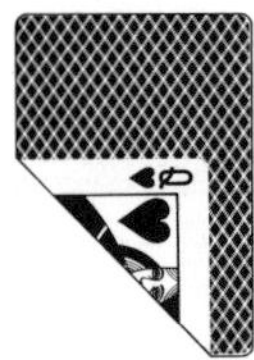

The game is moderately tight, you are in an early position, and there are two aces behind you, but they are not held by strong players. Be inclined to raise with this hand. (If you get reraised, meaning that you are against a probable pair of aces, you should usually fold.)

It is important to understand that if someone else has already limped in, you should usually not try to steal. However, an exception might be if a really tight player who probably has a medium pair — such as a pair of eights — limps in, and you know this person is capable of folding when you raise with something like a queen up. It is better to make this play against a person over whom you have good control. Furthermore, you normally should have a little something extra — like an ace in the hole.

One time not to steal with the highest card showing, even when you are not in an early position, is when the game is loose and you have terrible hole cards. Another time is when your upcard is duplicated elsewhere. Having your upcard duplicated presents three problems:

1. You must now worry about the opponent with the same upcard.
2. Your other opponents know that it is now harder for you to have the hand that you are representing.
3. Even if you do have this hand, it is harder to improve. Good players will react to your upcard being out elsewhere by "bombarding" you with chips.

Another important concept is that you can ante steal too much. Suppose you are in a game where at first you can steal the antes virtually every time. If you overdo it, your opponents will begin to realize what is happening, and this can create problems. First, you will be called a lot. Second, and even worse, some (if not all) of your opponents will start to reraise you. (Whether you should call these reraises is addressed later in this section.) Always remember, when ante stealing, that many players want to believe you are doing exactly that as it gives them an excuse to play.

So what's the conclusion as to how often you should ante steal? It is this: Steal slightly less frequently than what might appear to be correct. That is, throw away your worst hands (when you have the high card up) to keep your opponents trained to fold more often than they should. If possible, try to get a feel for what the optimum stealing frequency is for your game. Some games are very different from other games, in that you will be able to steal the antes much more often.

Following are some examples of minimum ante-stealing hands. The first is three high cards higher than the next highest upcard, such as

if no one else has a card as high as a seven. Other stealing hands are any kind of gut-shot draw and any kind of two-card flush draw, such as

if all of your cards are live and your upcard is big. However, keep in mind that to play this loose, your opponents must be folding a lot. Even if this is the case, it usually is best not to play these hands from an early position.

Now let's suppose that you are on a steal or a semi-steal, and someone reraises. Should you throw your hand away? The answer depends on what your cards are, what your opponent's upcard is, and on how the reraiser plays.

Suppose you raise with

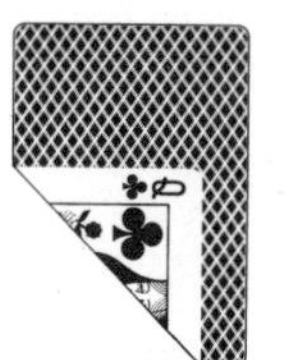  

and a seven reraises. You definitely would call. Similarly, if you have

you would call the seven. But if you raised with

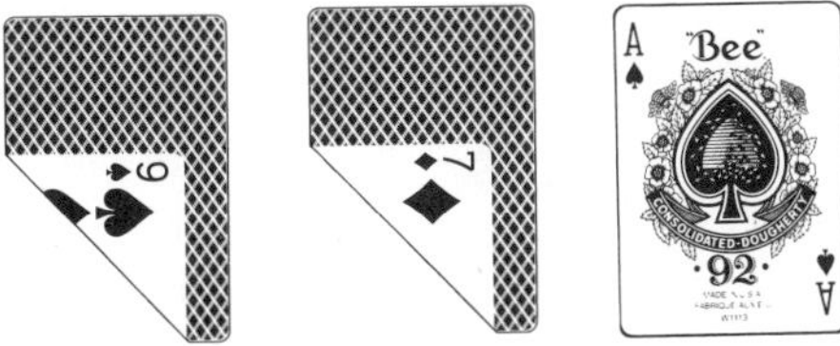

and a jack reraises, you should fold.

And if you have

and a king reraises, you probably should fold. However, if your opponent is prone to bluff, or if your hand is extremely live, you might call in this spot.

If you raise with

and a five reraises, you should call because you may have three overcards. But if you raised with a ten up (and something like seven-six in the hole) and a queen reraises, you should fold since you have no overcards.

Going back to the 9♣8♠A♥, should you ever not call the reraise from the five? The answer is that you should fold if you think you probably are against a big pair in the hole. This is one of those spots where knowledge of your opponent can be crucial in determining what play you should make. The earlier your positions, that is both you and your opponent, the more likely he will have a big pair in the hole.

Now suppose that after the low card brings it in, everyone folds and you are last. How often should you raise? The answer is that you should raise approximately 85 percent of the time against a typical player, but somewhat less against an expert. The other 15 percent of the time you usually should call. Fold only if:

1. You have absolutely nothing, and your opponent is extremely loose and aggressive. (If he checks a lot, you can play.) Or,
2. You have nothing, it is obvious, and your opponent is a very good player.

Here's an example of the second condition. A six brings it in. You have a seven up. Two sevens are out. It comes around to you, and you have absolutely nothing. Fold against a good player.

If you have next to nothing against a bad player, you should just call (when he is low and you are last) if this player will almost always call if you raise. Your call is correct because you are getting more than 4-to-1. Thus, folding is wrong just as raising would be. This is especially true against a very aggressive player who will either reraise or fold.

Suppose you are last and have:

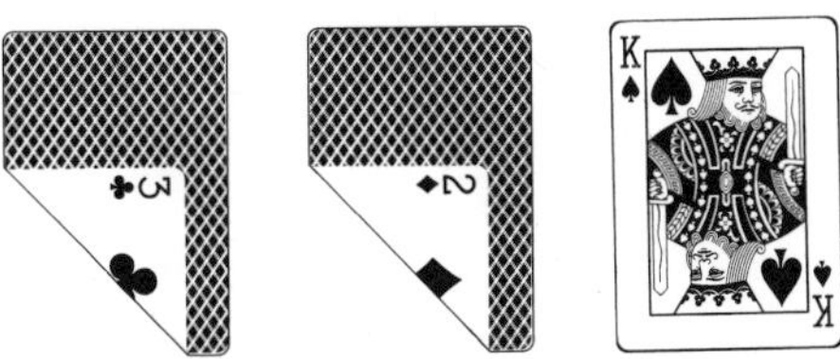

No other king is showing, a five brings it in, and everyone else folds. You should call a loose player but raise a tough player. However, if a couple of kings are out, you usually would just call against the tough player (although folding isn't that bad a play).

Even when your hand is terrible, the reason you would usually call instead of fold is that you may get the opportunity to catch one or two scare cards, which could allow you to win the pot with a bet. However, with your worst hands, whether you just call or raise, you must be prepared to give up quickly if your opponent bets. Failure to do this is one of the more costly (and common) mistakes.

Finally, we want to point out that ante stealing is part of winning stud play. If you believe that an ante steal will show a profit, then you should do it.

If you do try to steal more than you should, you still don't cost yourself much money as long as you know when to give it up. However, if you have raised on third street, get called, and you don't have much on fourth street, you should either be betting, or checking and folding. It is almost never right to be checking and calling in this spot. The only time that you should be doing this is when you have a pretty good hand but your opponent has caught the type of card that makes it correct to check and call. (There will be more discussion on this later in the text.) For example, if you raise with an ace, someone calls with a queen, and on fourth street they catch an offsuit five, you should always either bet or check and fold. Never check and call.

Three-of-a-Kind "Wired"

The best starting hand in seven-card stud is, of course, three-of-a-kind, also known as rolled up trips. You won't get this hand very often. It will occur on average only once in every 425 times that you are dealt in. Following is some advice on how to play these extremely good starting hands.

First, even though you have a very strong hand to begin with, it is not necessarily a "slowplaying" hand. To always slowplay strong hands, no matter what the situation, is a mistake in almost all forms of poker, including seven-card stud. Slowplaying rolled up trips is usually correct only in tight games. If there are loose, aggressive players behind you (and this type of opponent is fairly common at seven-card stud), they often will play and sometimes give a lot of action, even if you raise. In this situation, playing three-of-a-kind slow is definitely a mistake.

In reality, it usually doesn't matter very much how you play these hands if you are the first one in. If you have rolled up trips and several people have called, you definitely want to raise. However, if you are the first one in and hold three-of-a-kind, whether small or large, either calling or raising may be okay. The type of game, either loose or tight, or aggressive or passive, should be the deciding factor.

Some players will never raise with three-of-a-kind if they are up front. As just pointed out, this is not correct. One reason to raise in early position with this hand is that getting more money in the pot can "tie-on" other players. And no matter what your position, you should be more inclined to raise with rolled up trips if your trips are small. Remember, even though small rolled up trips are very strong, they often are beaten.

You usually should play small rolled up trips fast. Be sure to reraise if already raised, and frequently raise if there are many big cards behind you. Both of these raises will encourage a big pot. If it does turn out that you are looking at a big pair, your opponent will be anxious to get in an extra bet. Also, someone may reraise your small upcard with a big three-flush.

One reason to reraise a probable big pair with a rolled up hand is to make him think you have a bigger pair in the hole. The player holding the big pair almost always will play, and if he makes a hidden two pair, you will often get three bets out of him on either fifth or sixth street. If he pairs his board (not his door card), you usually will get two bets that round. The exception, of course, is if the original raiser shows an ace. Since you cannot have a higher pair in the hole, you may want to wait to raise so as not to arouse suspicion.

One thing you should consider when deciding whether to raise or reraise with three-of-a-kind is whether the raise may give your hand away. If it might, then be more inclined to call. An example of this would be if a queen raised and then an ace reraised. If you come over the top, you essentially are announcing your hand. By just calling, your opponents may think your most likely hand is a three-flush or a big pair in the hole, perhaps a pair of kings.

But there is an exception. If the table already has seen you make it three bets with something like a three-flush, then your opponents will not be as likely to think you are rolled up. If this is the case, a raise may still be the best play, especially since the pot has already gotten large enough that you might just as soon knock some players out.

If you did not raise coming in with rolled up trips, you usually should wait until fifth or even sixth street to start playing fast. However, keep in mind how the boards develop, and how timid your opposition is. Some timid opponents easily get scared out of betting on sixth street. This is especially true if you show something like a three-flush or perhaps even catch an ace. Against this type of player, waiting until sixth street to raise can be a mistake.

Playing Big Pairs

Besides rolled up trips, the other hand that you should just about always play is a pair of aces (even if both other aces are out). The only exception to playing a pair of aces is against several fast players if there is a raise and many calls before the action gets to you, and your aces are dead.

As for kings or queens, you should almost always play them as well. The time to throw them away is when you are positive that you are against a bigger pair or when your cards are dead. However, you should throw away a pair of tens or jacks if there are several overcards still to act behind you and if your kicker is weak.

Here is an example of the last concept. Suppose you have

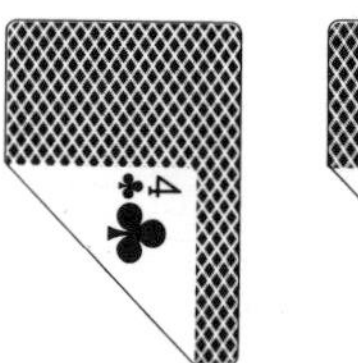

and there is a queen, a king, and an ace behind you. Normally, the correct play is to fold (unless the ante is very high).

One time that you should throw away a big pair is when the pot has been raised and reraised, and both players have higher exposed cards than your pair. In fact, you often should throw your hand away with just a raise and a call from the upcards we just described.

Here's an example. You have:

An ace raises and a queen calls. Unless you know these players very well (and know that there is a good chance that they do not have what they are representing), you probably should throw your hand away. In any case calling is extremely marginal.

An exception to this fold would be when you have a live overcard kicker (to go along with your live pair), higher than either of the upcards of the two active players. For example, instead of holding the J♥6♣J♠ above, suppose your kicker was the A♣, there were no other aces out, a queen raised, and a king reraised. In this case you should usually play and may even want to reraise again. Your reraise would be correct if you feel that there is a good chance that the player with the queen will fold, and this frequently will be the case.

If the player with the queen doesn't fold, this may require some creative play on your part to get him out of there. For example, it may be correct to check on fourth street (if they check to you the re-reraiser) and then to raise on fifth street, assuming the player with the king bets into you. This will almost always force an unimproved pair of queens to fold and will increase your chances of winning with jacks up.

If you have a big pair, but two or more *unduplicated* upcards higher than your pair are behind you, you probably should fold if your kicker is poor and you don't have a two-flush. However, if your kicker is good — either a live overcard or a live straight flush card — and is one of your downcards, go ahead and raise. (If reraised you should usually call.)

It may not be right to fold even if your kicker is weak. Raising might be correct. This will depend mostly on your opponents and whether your kicker is suited or not. The better they play or the more aggressive they are, the more inclined you should be to fold. (If you do raise and are reraised, you should almost always fold.) If your kicker is your upcard and is the highest card on board, then you usually should raise in this spot. Notice that this is consistent with our ante stealing requirements.

Notice that the additional out of a two-flush makes more hands playable. If you have a two-straight as well as a two-flush, that is even better. (Having an additional out, no matter what the form of poker, is often enough to make your hand significantly more valuable.)

As far as when to fold your big pairs after third street, you usually should give up if one of your opponents pairs his door card [See "Part Three: Miscellaneous Topics" — "Playing Against a Paired Door Card (on the Early Rounds)" on page 107.] or if by sixth street, one of your opponents has either a four-flush or a four-straight on board. Even though he may not have the straight or the flush, the chances that he already does have the hand — combined with the possibility that he will make the hand — make a fold on your part correct.

What you need to keep in mind when you hold a big pair is that these hands play best short-handed. Thus you usually should either raise or reraise and try to eliminate as many players as possible. And again keep in mind that your big pair is much more valuable if your hand is live.

Suppose you have a big pair, but there were several players in and your hand is dead. As we showed earlier it might be best to throw it away. And even if your hand was live, it would become correct to only call, not raise or reraise. Most experts don't know this but it is true!

There are two reasons. The first is strategic. If you don't raise you will have a better chance of knocking people out on a later round. The pot is smaller and there is a good chance that someone else will bet. This might allow you to raise or check-raise on fourth street. Additionally, if you bet out on fourth street, since there is less money in the pot, your opponents will be more inclined to fold because they are not getting as good a price. If you raised this would not be true.

Here's an example. Suppose you start with

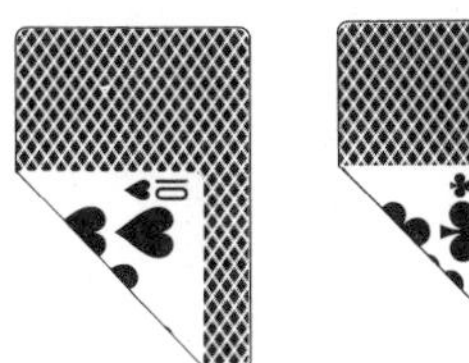

and catch a live ace on fourth street which you believe that your opponents may fear. You should now bet right out instead of trying for a check-raise. Because you didn't raise on third street they are more likely to incorrectly fold on fourth street, and you want them to do this.

The second reason is this: Let's say you are in a \$30-\$60 game and three players limp in for \$10 each. You are getting \$80-to-\$10 or 8-to-1 on your call. If you raise you will be getting \$140-to-\$30 or only 4⅔-to-1 assuming all active players call (which will almost always be the case). Even if there was no more betting after third street, it would be right to only call, rather than raise with some of these hands such as a big pair with a dead pair card. Your hand could easily have less than a one-in-five chance of winning, but still more than one-in-nine. Thus, calling would be correct while raising would theoretically cost you money.

If many players have limped in you should often just call with a big pair and be ready to throw it away on fourth street. For example, suppose after several people have limped in you also limp with a big pair. On fourth street someone pairs his door card and checks, but before the action gets to you someone else with a non-threatening board makes a full double size bet. You should probably throw your hand away. There is a good chance that you are beaten, maybe badly beaten, and there is not much money in the pot.

It can also be correct to "limp" with a big pair from an early position, but for completely different reasons. You might do this if most of the following is true:

1. By limping, you will convince most of your opponents that you do not have a big pair.
2. Because of the cards that are showing, your big pair is even stronger than normal.
3. You have a two-flush, and all your cards are live.
4. A player in late position is very aggressive, and he shows a high card.
5. Your limping in doesn't necessarily look like you are slowplaying a big hand.

An example of the second condition would be when you have an ace up (with an ace in the hole), there are just three players left behind you, and they all have a six up. An example of the fourth condition is when you have an ace up (with an ace in the hole), and a very aggressive player in late position has a queen up. Notice that if he plays you might be able to either reraise on third street or perhaps check-raise on fourth or fifth street.

There are two times when you may want to play big pairs deceptively because you don't want to give your hand away. (This is not the same as a slowplay or a limp.)

Here's an example. A king raised, a queen called, and you have:

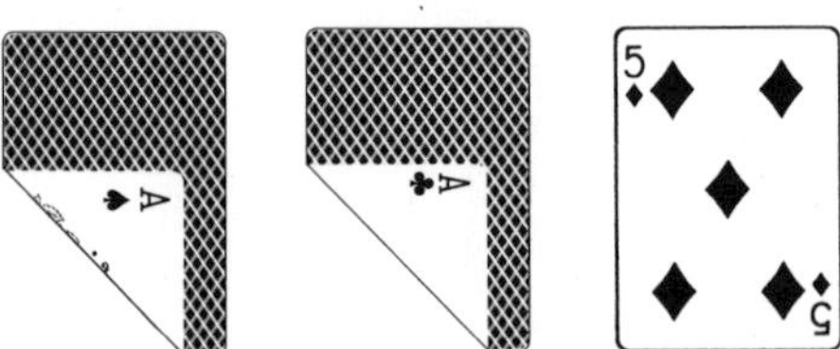

Since your aces are in the hole, you may only want to call in this spot. On the other hand, if you have been double raising a lot with three-flushes and have been noticed, then it would be correct to go ahead and reraise. One time when you *definitely would* reraise with this hand is if you think there is a possibility that you can get the initial raiser to throw his hand away. Suppose in the example just given, the order of the hands already in the pot was reversed; that is, the queen raised and the king called. Further, let's suppose that the person holding the queen is a very conservative player who might throw his hand away if you reraise. He will be afraid that if you don't have him beat, then the person holding the king just might. If the queen folds, you will be able to play heads-up against the king, who may not have a pair and probably has the third best hand. If the play doesn't work, that's okay. You still get more money in with the best hand. Another time your reraise is a must with a hand like buried aces in a three way pot would be when you think the initial raiser will reraise you to knock the third player out.

Here's another example of deceptive play. You are the low card with two aces in the hole, and a king — someone not in a steal position — brings it in for a raise, and no one else is in the pot. You probably should just call and hope to get a raise in later. If he is in a steal position be inclined to raise. He may automatically reraise thinking that you are just defending against his possible steal. Now just call and look to raise again on a later street, probably fifth street.

One undesirable situation that sometimes develops is that you will raise with a split big pair and a higher card behind you will reraise. If your kicker is higher than his upcard, you should call and be prepared to go to the river.

You can also call the raise if your kicker is a live straight flush card. (However, if you catch blanks on fourth and fifth street you should probably give it up.) Without a quality kicker, fold immediately if it is unlikely that this person would raise you with anything but a higher pair. Otherwise call.

Here's an example. You have:

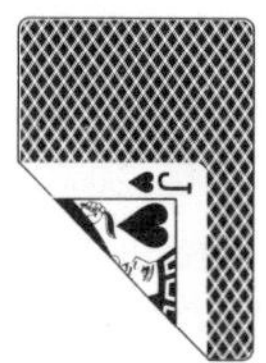  

You raise, a person holding a queen reraises, and this is the kind of person who has to have at least two queens to make this play. You should now fold. If you call in this spot, it can be a very costly mistake, especially if it compounds itself on the later streets. (However, if your kicker was a live ace or king you must call his reraise — and in fact call all the way up to sixth street in most cases as long as your opponent shows no improvement. If your kicker was a live, suited nine or ten, you should still call and then make a decision on fifth street as to whether it is correct to continue.)

Reraising the Possible Bigger Pair

It is sometimes correct to reraise on third street with a big pair when a higher upcard has raised. This is especially true against a player over whom you have good control, or against someone whose upcard is duplicated elsewhere. It is also the correct play against an aggressive player who is apt to have little.

For example, suppose an ace comes in for a raise and you have:

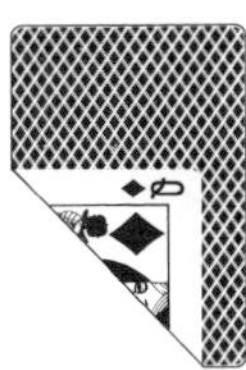 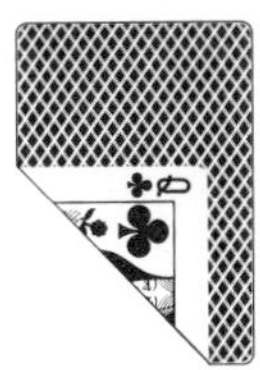 

If no other queen is out and one of the three conditions mentioned above is favorable, make it two bets. If one of your queens is out, you still can make it two bets if your opponent is smart enough to originally raise with an ace high only, but not tricky enough to reraise without having two aces. (This is partly what we mean by having good control over an opponent.) If it does go to three bets, you then can assume you are against two aces (or two kings in the hole).

But there are problems with reraising the ace:

1. There is a good chance that if you don't raise, the ace will bet into you the whole pot, which will give you a great edge if he doesn't have aces.
2. Your opponent can always pair aces later on, even if he doesn't have them to start with. Consequently, this is a close decision.

The deciding factor: Is your raise required to get the pot heads-up? If you are in late position and there is no one between you and the ace, then the raise may not be necessary since there is a good chance that you will be heads-up anyway. On the other hand, if there are several players still to act behind you, a reraise is now mandatory strategy if you play the hand at all. (If your opponent now reraises indicating two aces, you don't fold the pair of queens. The pot is now large enough that you should call and be prepared to go to the river.)

It is important to realize that a player who raises with an ace, without necessarily having aces, yet who does require a decent hand to make this raise, is someone you need to be concerned with. Put another way, your opponent has a pretty good chance of either already having a pair of aces or improving to a good hand, which could be a pair of aces or better. So it is very dangerous to reraise someone who has an ace up if he is playing well.

On the other hand, the play of reraising a possibly higher pair *other* than aces is frequently clearly correct. In fact, when your kicker is higher than the pair your opponent is representing, to *not* reraise is usually a terrible play as long as only the two of you (plus the bring-in) are in the pot to that point. Even if you are sure he isn't bluffing it is usually better to reraise (to get it heads-up and to take control of the hand) as long as your cards are live and your kicker is high. (See "Part One: Third Street" — "More Discussion on Calling Versus Raising" on page 54.)

Playing Small and Medium Pairs

The first thing to keep in mind when you have a small pair is that these hands are much worse than big pairs. A pair of eights, for instance, is significantly weaker than a pair of queens. This is especially true if your kicker is small.

Here's an example. Suppose a deuce brings it in, and you are next with:

Automatically playing this holding is a big mistake.

To determine whether a small or medium pair is playable when you are not in a steal position, you must consider the following six factors:

1. How high your kicker is.
2. Whether your cards are all live. (If one of your pair cards is out you should rarely play. If one of your kickers is out, it still might be worth it, but not if two of them are gone.)
3. What the other upcards are.
4. What the game is like.
5. Whether your pair is in the hole. (It is usually better if the pair is in the hole, but the reverse may be true if you have an ace or a king kicker.)
6. Whether you also have a two-card flush (or less importantly a two-card straight), especially if the flush cards are live. (Also, it is slightly better for the two-card flush to be in the

hole, and it is even better if you have a two-card straight flush.)

The two most important factors are the size of your kicker and whether your cards are all live.

So how high does your kicker need to be? The answer is that it should be higher than any card on board (but if it isn't an ace or a king it's not that strong).

Here's an example. A deuce brings it in. You have

and all your cards are live. The hand is certainly worth playing for the bring-in. If it is a full bet, the hand is still worth playing, but whether *you* should make it a full bet is debatable. What the game is like should influence your decision. Obviously, if the game is very tight and you think you have some chance to steal, be more inclined to make it a full bet.[2] Also be more inclined to raise if you feel that this will get you heads-up. (See "Part One: Third Street" — "More Discussion on Calling Versus Raising" on page 54.)

In addition, you should frequently reraise higher upcards. This is correct if you can get it heads-up, your cards are live, one of their upcards is gone, or there is some chance they don't have what they are representing.

The way you judge this last condition is not only by the type of player it is, but also the cards on the board. If a person raises where he has reason to believe that he can get away with a steal — perhaps he has the highest card or perhaps there are a lot of duplicated cards — then there is some chance to believe that he

---

[2] If the game is tight it might be best to find another game.

doesn't have it. But if a jack on your right raises, and there is a queen on your left, this is not the situation that we are talking about. First of all, he probably has the two jacks or some other good hand, and second, you are not necessarily going to get it heads-up. But if you are almost sure you can get it heads-up, and there is either some doubt about his having the pair or one of his upcards is out, you just reraise (with that ace kicker).

Another question that comes up is how long should you stay with a small or medium pair? This depends on what you think you have to beat, how much money is in the pot, and how the hand will be played from that point on. Automatically folding on fourth or fifth street when you haven't improved is not correct. There certainly will be times when you should go all the way to the river (even though you have not improved). There is further discussion on this topic throughout the text.

Now suppose you have a medium pair, such as two nines. If there are no cards or only one card behind you higher than your nines, go ahead and raise, no matter what your upcard is. Another time that you should raise is when you have a concealed small or medium pair and the highest upcard, and you are the first one in. Again notice that this is consistent with our ante stealing strategy. Be happy if you just get the antes.

Having the highest upcard with your small pair in the hole has certain advantages. It allows you to represent a different hand than what you actually have. Plus it makes it easier to make the best two pair. If you get raised when you hold a medium pair and a high kicker that is your upcard, you should usually call. However, if you get raised and reraised, you should usually fold against this double bet. As mentioned previously, the exception would be when you have a live overcard kicker (to go along with your live pair) higher than either of the upcards of the two active players.

If it is raised ahead of you and you have a concealed pair lower than the upcard of the raiser, you usually should fold if there are any players behind you with unduplicated upcards higher than the raiser's upcard. One reason why you should fold in this spot is that you can be raised again. Another reason is that since the raiser was looking at higher upcards and still raised, he probably has a real hand.

For example, suppose the raiser has a queen up and there is a king behind him. It is very likely that you are looking at a pair of queens, as opposed to a steal hand. Many players will also have a high three-flush in this spot but that is also a real hand. Thus, you should throw away most pairs below queens, especially if the king is yet to act.

If you have a pair and one of your pair cards is out, you should fold if it appears that someone has a higher pair. An exception to this is if your kicker is higher than the highest card on board. But remember, even this situation is not so great, unless your kicker is an ace or a king. Keep in mind that you have a dead card and you must improve. This means that if your decision is close and you are against a strong player, you should consider folding even with the higher kicker.

The only time that a small pair with one of the pair cards out is automatically playable is when you are in a good position to steal. (However, this does not imply that you *should* normally play a low pair with no kicker just because your hand is live.)

If there are one or two higher cards behind you, but the six factors listed earlier in this section are favorable, and no one has yet voluntarily entered the pot, you should at least call with your pair if you have a live quality kicker. But frequently you should go ahead and raise whether or not your kicker is up. The time that this raise would be especially correct is when you are against weak players over whom you have good control.

Here's an example. Suppose you have:

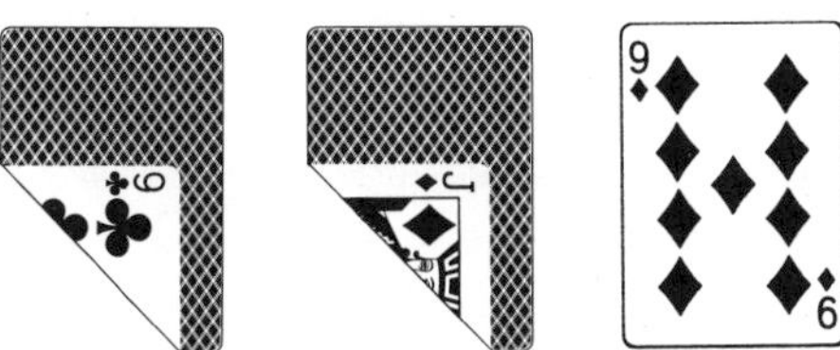

Your cards are live, no one is yet in the pot, but behind you is an ace and a king. (Notice that the J♦ is a straight flush card.) You should usually raise.

You can't fold the pair of nines with a suited jack if your cards are live even if you thought that there was a good chance that the player with the ace up does have two aces. So it is better to raise yourself. And in this case if you are reraised you have to call. If your jack was not a straight flush card then the right play is to raise, and if you get reraised, usually fold.

When you have the two nines (no matter what your kicker), one reason to consider raising with two overcards behind you is if they both fold you might get to charge a bad player with a smaller pair. Of course, this assumes that there are additional players behind the overcards.

But suppose you have

in this same situation. If you are going to play, you should only call, and folding is probably the correct option because getting the big cards out does you little good if a hand like two sixes stays in.

If there are three or four cards behind you higher than your pair, usually fold. Consider calling only with a high kicker or if your kicker is a straight flush card that's very live on both straights and flushes. (Or if you are in a game with a very high ante.)

Remember, when evaluating pairs on third street, you must consider the six factors mentioned. Every time you pick up a medium pair, you need to think about whether you have a two-flush or a two-straight, how live your hand is, and how high your kicker is. For instance, if you are sure that your opponent has a big pair — such as two queens — and you have a small or medium pair, for your call to be correct, you need (among other things) either an ace or a king kicker. A straight flush kicker is usually not good enough in this spot unless you are in a game with a very high ante. (If you raised and were *reraised*, the straight flush kicker now makes your hand — along with the extra money in the pot — good enough to keep playing.)

Also, when you make this call, your kicker usually needs to be in the hole. Otherwise you will have to lead all the way, thus showing weakness when you check. In addition, with your kicker in the hole, you can catch three cards to give you a hidden hand, as opposed to two cards if you have a wired pair.

Here's an example. You have:

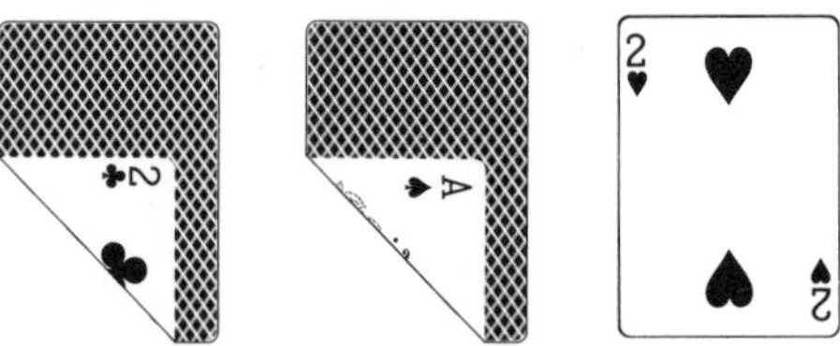

It is generally worth it to go all the way against a probable pair lower than aces in a heads-up situation, providing that your opponent does not improve and your cards remain live.

If it is raised ahead of you, the raiser is not in a steal position, and your kicker is live but small, you should fold even if there are not threatening cards behind you. The only times that it is correct to play a small pair with a small kicker is as an ante steal or when you know you can get in cheaply. If you think there is a reasonable chance that you will be raised, it is best to throw the hand away.

If a high card raises in front of you and you have a live pair with an even higher live kicker, you should usually reraise *if* you can get it heads-up. Otherwise, normally call. If your kicker is a straight flush card and you anticipate a multiway pot, you can also call.

If you raise with a medium pair, a smaller card reraises, and you know this player has a bigger pair in the hole, you should call. That's right; calling is correct! The reason for continuing with the hand is that, except for the last card, your opponent cannot make two pair without you, knowing it. (See "Part Three: Miscellaneous Topics" — "Playing Two Pair Against a Hidden Big Pair" on page 104.)

Playing Three-Flushes

Another set of quality starting hands are the three-flushes, and not all three-flushes are the same. Some are virtually always playable, while others should usually be discarded. A few can be played very aggressively, while others can be played only if the cost is kept to a minimum. Some three-flushes play well heads-up, while most prefer a crowd. As you can see, correct strategy for three-flushes is quite varied.

To begin with, there are four things to consider in determining how and whether you play your starting three-flush. They are:

1. What your position is.
2. What your door card is.
3. How many of your cards are out.
4. How high your cards are.

What seems to be small differences in these four parameters can greatly impact the approach to playing these hands. For instance, if you have a three-flush and none of your suit is out, your hand is almost always playable, unless you have three small cards and it is three bets to you, or two high cards raise and reraise.

Here's an example. Suppose you hold

and no other clubs are showing. This hand is usually playable, unless one of the two exceptions just mentioned is applicable.

If three or more of your suit are out, your three-flush is just about always unplayable. Exceptions are if the hand can be played as an ante steal, or if it has value other than the three-flush aspect, such as a possible straight draw or high cards.

Here's an example of a totally worthless hand. Suppose you have

and there are three diamonds, as well as a ten and a five, out. This hand is virtually always unplayable.

If in the above case two of your suit were out but no tens, fives, or deuces, the hand becomes barely playable as long as it doesn't cost too much. However, the hand is unplayable if you think you may be heads-up against a high pair.

In fact, even if your cards are completely live, if you are *heads-up* against a raiser and your three-flush contains all small cards, you might want to fold, especially if you are against a good player. But if the raiser may not have anything, it is clearly at least a call.

Thus, if you hold the <u>T♦5♦</u>2♦ and you are going to be heads-up against a raiser with a probable large pair, your hand is generally not worth playing. This is true even if your flush draw and pair cards are live. On the other hand, even if almost all the tens, fives, and deuces are gone, but your flush cards are completely live, you usually should play in a *multiway* pot.

If you are the first one in and you have a three-flush with a high card showing, then you should usually, but not always, enter the pot with a raise. This is true even if there is one higher card still to act behind you as this allows you to mix up your three-flushes with your high-pair raises, creating some deception in your play. If you do have the highest card on board, it is unlikely that you will be reraised.

Next, suppose you hold a big straight flush draw, such as:

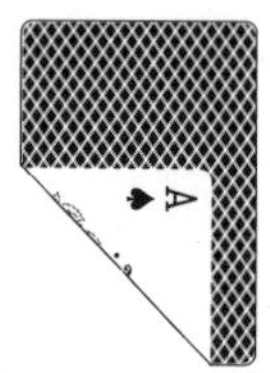

You probably want to raise so that you can narrow the field in case you make a high pair. But if you don't raise, or if you can't thin the field, having a lot of opponents when you hold this hand is also good. When you have a high three-flush with straight potential and you are the first one in, normally raise only if there is no more than one card higher behind you. With a small three-card straight flush, however, you should not raise unless a few players are already in.

If you have a three-flush with one card higher than the raiser's door card, then you should always at least call, unless your hand is not very live. This is true even if you are fairly sure that you will be heads-up against a probable big pair.

If you have a three-flush, and two big cards ahead of you raise and reraise, you can play only if you have at least one card higher than the two big cards. Here's an example. Suppose a ten raises, a queen reraises, and you have:

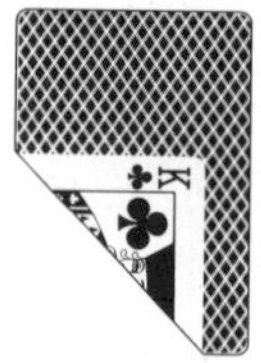
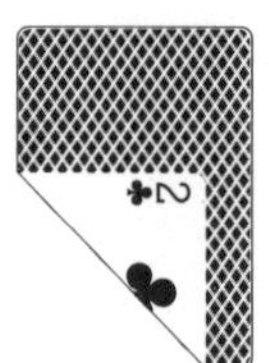

Since you hold a king, go ahead and play as long as your cards are live. If there is just a raise and a call, then you can play any three-flush if your cards are live. However, if your three-flush is small and two of your suit are out, you usually should throw your hand away. To play a three-flush with two of your suit elsewhere on the board usually requires big cards.

Sometimes it is correct to raise with your three-flush even when you cannot steal the antes. For instance, suppose someone has just called the bring-in. If you have two overcards and at least a medium card up, you can raise. The reason for raising is that if you pair one of your overcards, you would prefer to be heads-up. It may even be right to raise with just one overcard, particularly if it is an ace or a king. (There will be more discussion on this later in the text.)

Here's an example. Suppose you have

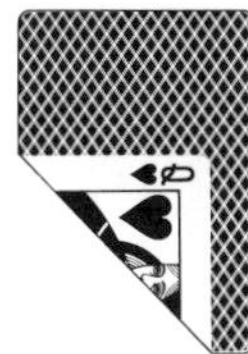

and someone has limped in with a ten up. You probably want to raise. If the Q♥ was a small heart instead, it still might be correct to raise in an attempt to get heads-up.

If someone has already raised, you have two overcards, and one of them is up, you can go ahead and reraise. This is particularly valid if you think your opponent may not have what he is representing, or if he is the type of player who can throw a pair away. It might still be okay to make this play when both overcards are in the hole or when you have only one overcard, as long as it is either an ace or a king.

Playing Three-Straights

The next class of starting hands that we will examine are the three-straights. Obviously, they are not usually as good as the three-flushes. However, three-straights *in the right spots* can be profitable hands.

When deciding whether to play a three-straight, you must consider the following eight factors:

1. How high your cards are.
2. How live your straight cards are.
3. How live your pair cards are.
4. Whether you have a two-flush.
5. The other cards on board.
6. Who is already playing.
7. How much it is to you, that is, whether you can play for the bring-in, one bet, or two bets.
8. The ability of your opponents.

Needless to say, the more favorable these factors are, the more you should be inclined to play. In fact, if the factors are extremely favorable, you may even want to raise.

Sometimes with a three-card straight it is worth calling one full bet, but not two full bets, cold. Here's an example. Suppose you have:

One seven and one queen are out, but no jacks or sixes are gone. Now the queen raises and an ace calls. Go ahead and call for a full bet. However, if the ace had reraised, you should throw the hand away.

By the way, this hand is not as good as it appears. This is because it looks as though *two* queens are out. So if you catch a jack, you now have just five straight cards left. This is one of the reasons why this hand should not be played in this situation for two bets.

Occasionally, however, a three-straight can be played for two cold bets. This occurs when the conditions outlined are favorable and particularly if you have high cards (overcards to your opponents' probable pairs) and/or a two-flush.

Keep in mind that when you have close decisions with hands like straight draws you should always consider how well your opponents play. For example, if your opponent is the type of player who gets "married" to a high pair, you know that if you make your hand you will get paid off all the way, even if it is obvious that you have made a straight. So this is a small extra enticement to call, as long as you don't go overboard.

Now suppose you have a small, three-card "gut-shot" straight, such as:

When is it correct to play this hand? The main thing to consider is how live your cards are (especially the eight in this case). Also, be more inclined to play if everybody else has small cards and you have an overcard. However, even with this being said, these hands usually are not playable. (For exceptions see the section on "Playing Weak Hands" on page 66.) And three-straights with *two* gaps generally should not be played at all.

The problem with gaps is that unless your cards are high, you must catch that specific "gut" card. And don't forget that you may make your straight and still lose.

Here's an example. Suppose you have:

You must catch an eight. But if you are holding

there is no specific card that you must catch to become part of your straight.

If your gut shot is bigger, such as

you should be somewhat more inclined to play, since your straight, and more importantly your pairs, will probably be bigger.

If you have a consecutive three-straight but three of your straight cards are dead, you definitely should not play unless you have a good chance to steal the antes. If two of your straight cards are dead, you probably should not play, especially if other considerations (such as how high your cards are) appear unfavorable.[3]

But there is still more to consider. Let's assume that a card you need is shown by someone who has stayed in on third street. This means it is likely that he has additional cards you need. For example, if an opponent has a ten up, he may have another ten or other cards — such as a nine or a jack — that you may need.

If an opponent just calls the bring-in, you have at least two cards higher than his upcard, and there is no more than one higher card behind you, then it is okay to raise with your three-straight. If there are two or more high cards behind you, play it cautiously. That is, don't raise. In addition, it is rarely correct to reraise with a three-straight. (One exception is covered in the chapter on "Playing Big Cards Against a Medium Pair" on page 113.) Another time to reraise occurs when you think the original raiser may be semi-bluffing. (See the chapter on "Defending Against the Possible Ante Steal" on page 101.)

Three-straights made up of small cards are not very good hands. They generally should only be played when you can get in cheaply and when your hand is live, or when you have a chance to steal the antes. One of their problems is that by the time you have the multiway action that you think you like, you can make your hand and lose to a higher straight or flush. Play them with caution.

---

[3] Keep in mind that with an open end three-card-straight the cards directly next to them (i.e. six and ten when you have nine-eight-seven) are more important than the other two straight cards (i.e. five and jack), as they are more likely to be needed.

More Discussion on Calling Versus Raising

We want to pause here and talk a little more about calling versus raising. This is a decision that constantly comes up which most players don't handle very well.

Earlier we talked about seemingly good hands that because of the multiway nature of the situation you should only call with because they had less than a one-in-five chance of winning, but still more than one-in-nine. Depending on the situation, that can be a lot of hands, perhaps as high as 20 percent in unraised pots.

Let's suppose that you are again in that $30-$60 game, three players call, and you are last. You should call liberally because you are getting 8-to-1 from the pot. But you shouldn't raise with many hands since you are only getting 3-to-1 on your raise. Furthermore, some of the hands that appear to be worth raising really aren't because the future action may be detrimental to them. Consequently, if it has become apparent that you can't get heads-up, you should limp with many hands that other players will frequently raise with.

For instance, if a deuce brings it in, three people call the bring-in, and you are last, when you don't fold you should limp at least two-thirds of the time. In these spots the typical pro will probably raise two-thirds of the time if he plays his hand. But he's wrong because he cannot stop players from coming in behind him since he is already last.

Here's an example. A deuce brings it in, a five calls, a seven calls, and a nine calls. You have

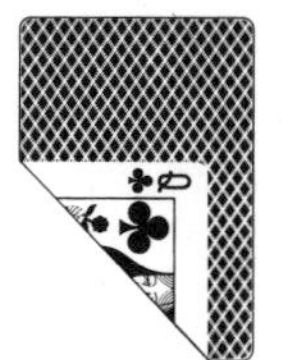  

and are next to the bring-in. You should just call. There is little to be gained by raising. If instead of the 8♦ your kicker was the

giving you a straight flush card, you could go ahead and raise because your hand plays much better multiway. However, if one of your queens was dead, you would be back to just calling even if you held a straight flush kicker.

On the other hand, you should in general raise with more hands than most people do as long as the pot is not multiway and you are not last to act (before the bring-in). This includes most of your playable pair hands, especially if your cards are live, because getting heads-up is almost always better than not getting heads-up. Many people think that a hand like

 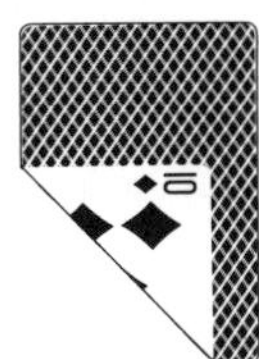 

is the kind of hand where you want to see what you catch on fourth street. But if you hold this hand and there is a player with a nine up behind you, it is better to make it a full bet and have him reraise you than it would be to just call and have him make it a full bet if this allows callers behind him, and you now have to play multiway. If that happened you would be in bad shape. But heads-up, your pair of fives with a ten kicker against a pair of nines, is not in that bad of shape.

Now we are not saying that you should call if a nine raises and you have 5♥T♦5♣. In fact, you should frequently fold. Only call if everyone else is out and you are fairly sure that it will be a heads-up pot. We are just saying that you should make the original raise yourself if your biggest fear would be a reraise from a nine showing.

So whether or not you should raise often has to do with how effective your raise will be in knocking people out. And this includes some hands that typical players will just call with.

There are very few hands where you don't gain much by knocking people out.

is an example. But they are few and far between. Because of the "dead" money in the pot (the antes and bring-in) most hands do better against one opponent. To take an extreme example, say an ace raises, you have

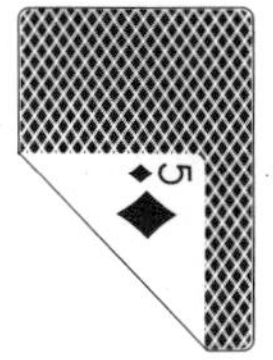

(notice that the king is up), and you think that the ace may be stealing. You may be better off reraising in an attempt to limit the pot to the two of you. Allowing other people to play can easily be more costly than the extra bets risked against a possible pair of aces.

Continuing with this example, suppose there is a queen behind you. It is important to knock him out if he has two queens because the ace might be bluffing, and most important, if you make two pair and the queens also makes two pair, but the ace does not, you can still lose. This is why it is important to have the king up. If an ace raises and a king reraises, it will be very difficult for anyone with two queens to call.

On the other hand, suppose in this situation your hand was:

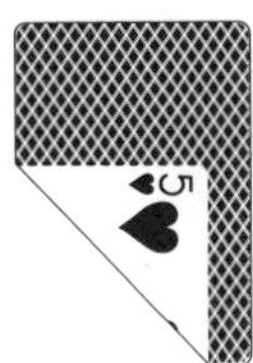
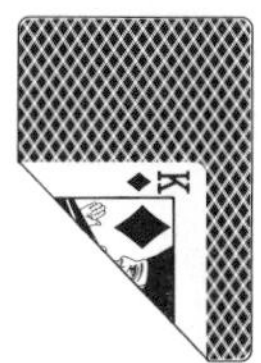

That is, you really do have two kings.

It is now not nearly as important to knock someone out because if your first opponent has aces you still have to make at least two pair to win. Now the player with the queens will have to catch a third one to beat you. Notice that we have described a situation where you would want to knock out the player behind you if you only have a pair of fives, but would be willing to let him play if you have a pair of kings. As you can see, seven-card stud can be a very complex game.

If you think you have the best pair, whether it is showing or not, someone else raises and several people call, you should frequently not reraise if no one will be knocked out. Furthermore, your decision of whether to take it to two full bets should be influenced by your position. Obviously, if a queen raises, a jack calls, and you are next with a pair of kings, you should reraise to get everyone out behind you. But if you were last and only the bring-in was behind you, you are probably better off just calling. (This is something that virtually no one else will do.) The difference is not the number of people in the pot, but the number of people that still might come into the pot.

You need to be aware of how different hands do against different numbers of players. Let's say you hold a hand that does much better heads-up than multiway. You should try to get heads-up if possible. If you know you can't get it heads-up, you have to consider how well this hand will do multiway. Now you have to decide whether to call or to fold. Typical players will often just call in this spot. They will call when the expert raises, and they will call when the expert folds.

The hands that you want to play heads-up are pairs, high cards without pairs, and high straight draws — especially if they are higher than everyone else. For example,

definitely plays well heads-up against a seven. If a seven raises and you have this hand, it is an almost automatic reraise. If a seven raises and a four calls, now it's close, but it still might be worth a reraise. But if a seven raises, a four calls, and a trey calls, you should only call. One other time not to raise a seven with that Q♣J♥T♠ is when you are against a player who will only raise with a small card up when he has a big pair in the hole. You don't want to go heads-up against a higher pair.

(By the way, this last example illustrates one reason why you often raise with a hand like:

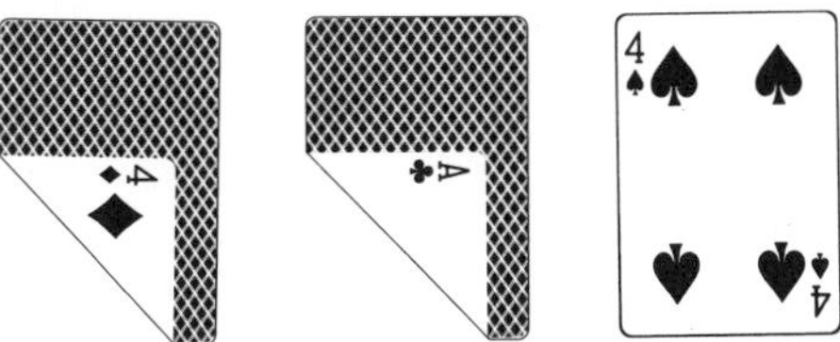

If you didn't, your opponents could almost always correctly put you on a big pair in the hole when you raise with a small card up. Thus, you would be giving away too much information.)

To finish this chapter we want to discuss two times when you should limp in early. The first time is when you have a hand that's much better off multiway than heads-up against an overcard. For instance, suppose you have:

There is an ace and a king behind you, and a lot of low cards behind them. Here you clearly should not raise. The problem is that if you make it a full bet, one of the big cards can make it two full bets, meaning a heads-up pot, when you don't have an overcard.

It would be different if you had

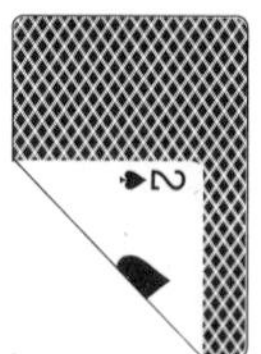

and there was a jack and a nine behind you. You could go ahead and raise. Even if you are reraised it is okay since you have an overcard.

The second time that you want to limp up front is when you have a hand that prefers to get in as cheaply as possible because you are willing to give it up on fourth street if you don't catch a perfect card. But if you catch just right you could like it a lot. An example would be a three-card-straight or a three-card-flush when a couple of your cards are out. There still are enough cards left that fourth street could come good, and it is well worth trying if you can get in cheaply. Another example would be a live small pair with a straight flush kicker. (Note: If you are raised on third street after limping in you may want to fold.)

More Discussion on Playable Hands

As we pointed out earlier in the text, you must always take into account the cards that are out. For example, if a queen raises and another queen calls, you should be very inclined to play against them because it is so likely that two pair will win, especially if they both catch bad cards on fourth street. So when you take into account the cards that are out, you don't just consider how live your hand is, you also consider how the other upcards may impact your opponents' hands as well.

Here's an extreme example. Suppose a deuce brings it in, a trey folds, a nine calls, another nine calls, you're next with

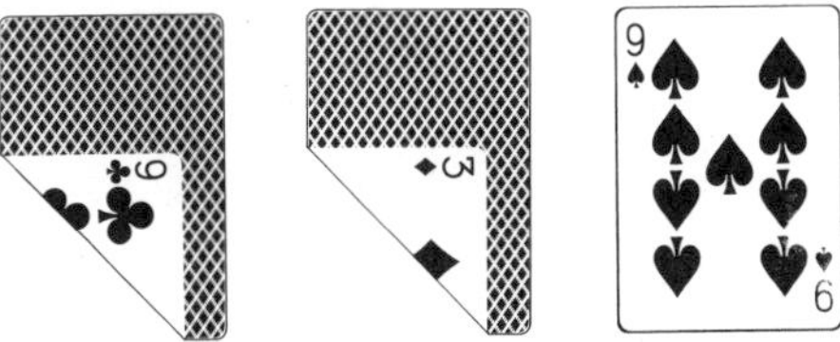

and behind you are an eight and two sixes. You should fold. Not only is your hand dead, but one of the limpers with a nine up could easily have a hand like jack-ten-nine which your hand won't play well against. Also you have too many opponents.

Here's an example from the opposite point of view. Suppose you have:

You are against someone who holds a pair of aces, and one of the remaining aces as well as one of the aces' kicker is out. If you deal out all the cards you will beat the aces approximately 45 percent of the time (depending on exactly what the other upcards are) which is more than enough to make your hand playable heads-up.

But your hand is actually better than this. If you make an open pair (except for maybe your door card), your opponent will keep coming. But if he makes an open pair you can fold. Furthermore, your opponent might check on a later street giving you a free card.

So if you have live cards and your opponent has a dead card to his big pair it is correct for you to play heads-up with a hand like a small pair and a straight flush card. However, this same hand in a three-way pot becomes a disaster because if you make two pair you will frequently beat the player with the big pair, but lose to the third player. This means that you should frequently reraise in this spot if you believe that the extra bet will get the pot heads-up.

You may want to pause and think about what we have just said. We are suggesting that with a small pair and a straight flush kicker you should reraise a big pair, not a possible big pair, but a definite big pair, if one of your opponent's pair cards is already out, your hand is live, and no one else is in. If this is what you have to do to get this pot heads-up, then by all means go ahead and do it.

Here's another example. Suppose a ten raises, you have

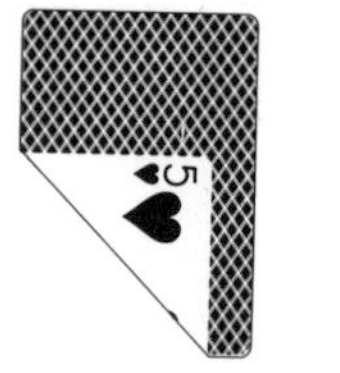
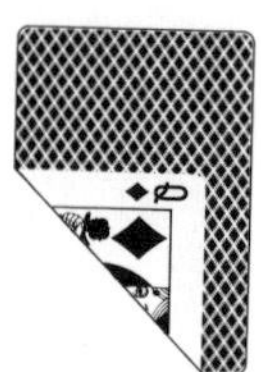

and a jack has already called. You should usually fold. The exception would be if you were last and your cards were live. If the jack had not played, your hand becomes playable and you should at least call.

If, however, you were between the ten and the jack you could try to make it heads-up for one extra bet. This is an expense that you should not worry about. Thanks to your reraise, your hand has become playable. However, if there were many high cards behind you, instead of reraising, you should again fold.

If a ten raises, a jack calls, and a seven calls you shouldn't play 5♥Q♦5♠ unless you had a two-flush, every card you need is live, and you are against bad players. The problem is that your chances of winning are going down faster than the size of the pot is going up. (If you make two small pair it is very unlikely that it will be good enough to win.)

So the fact is that a hand like 5♥Q♦5♠ should usually only be played heads-up. Many players think that you would rather play these hands multiway hoping to catch a perfect card, but that's not really true. A large part of your profit comes from winning with two small pair. This contribution pretty much disappears once it becomes multiway.

What you must do at the beginning of any hand is to look at your three cards and decide if your hand has been helped or hurt by the cards that are out. You must also take into account how many players you are likely to be up against. For example, if you have

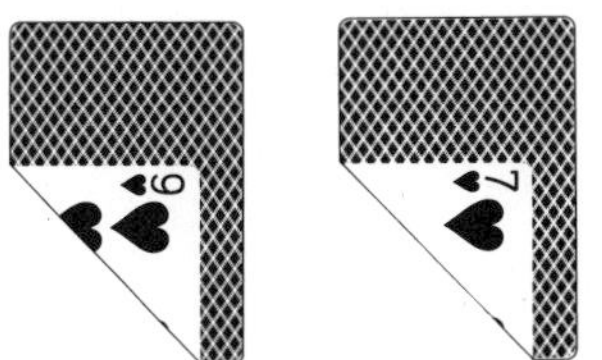

all you normally do is see how many other hearts are in the other players' hands. However, if you have a medium high three-straight, all types of information can change your decision. You need to consider what the upcards are, whether your cards are dead, how many people you will be up against, whether their

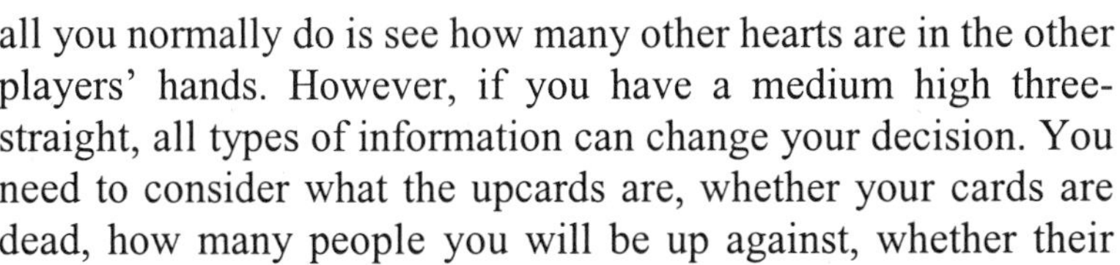

cards are dead, will hitting a pair figure to win, what will likely happen on the next round, and who will act first on the next round.

So while some hands don't require much thinking, other hands do, since there are all kinds of information that can change your strategy. However, you should always be looking to play as many hands as you profitably can. If you can find six extra hands an hour to play and average winning $3 on each of them, that is $18 an hour additional profit. On the other hand if you play these marginal hands poorly, and it costs you $2 a hand, then you are looking at a $30 an hour swing from what an expert would do. It doesn't do you any good to play them if you don't play them right.

This is why some players do very well at stud, and why the best stud players can make a little more than the best hold 'em players. In hold 'em, only a few hands can change from being right to play to being wrong to play based on the situation. Perhaps 10 percent of the hands are debatable, and whether or not you should play them depends on how many people are in the pot, and on how good the other players are. But in seven-card stud, at least twice as many starting hands are susceptible to these changes because the upcards and number of players against you makes more of a difference.

Typical players, some of whom are even small winners, do not do a good job of adjusting the value of their hands to the particular situation. However, the great players, some of whom appear to play very loose, are well aware of these concepts and are constantly adjusting the value of their hand (on all streets as well as on the first three cards) to make their playing decisions.

Randomizing Your Play

There is something else about the cards that are out that can swing your decisions. It is that they are a good randomizing device for your deceptive plays. Specifically, on third street (and fourth street) instead of making your deceptive plays with unacceptable hands, you can make them with reasonable hands. The cards that are out or the number of players in the pot can help you do something other than what appears to be normal.

Suppose for various technical reasons you determine that it is proper strategy to just call with a pair of kings in a particular situation when one of the kings is up. Three things will usually result. First, most of the players won't put you on that hand as it is being played. Second, once your hand is exposed, all but the best players will simply think that you were merely trying to be tricky that hand. And third, when you call in some other spot with a king up — perhaps you have a three-flush — your opponents will worry that you have kings. Virtually no one will realize that you flat called because of your position or the upcards. For example, you would just call with kings when there are a few people already in, and one or two of your cards are dead.

So if your opponents don't realize that these factors are part of your decision making process, they will think that you are just mixing it up for random reasons rather than real reasons. That is, and this is very important, you will get your randomness without actually having to be random. In fact, in seven-card stud none of your decisions need to be based on randomness as they might be in other games. You can mix it up enough for reasons that virtually no one understands.

Playing Weak Hands

You must realize that many players get out of line on third street. Suppose you start with:

An ace raises, a king calls, and now you call. You should have folded!

Assuming that you incorrectly called, suppose that on fourth street the ace catches a jack, the king catches a ten, and you catch a seven. It is again wrong to call. You have caught only enough to "suck you in." Your hand has not improved enough to make it profitable to continue playing. But notice that your error on third street has caused you to make an additional compounding error on fourth street that can become very expensive once the hand is over.

You need to keep in mind that only the very best players can get away with getting slightly out of line on third street, especially for a full bet. Most players compound the error later on.

If, however, the third street bet is only the bring-in and it is unlikely that you will be raised, things are a little different. In fact, many good players probably play a little too tight in this spot. There are a lot of hands that you can play if it's cheap, if your hand is live, and if it has the potential to make something big.

(If you do play a weak hand for the bring-in and are raised, you usually should now fold and save the rest of the bet. There are two reasons for this:

1. It is costing you more money.

2. The fact that the pot has been raised has diminished the value of your hand. Conversely, if you encounter tough players who are apt to make their fold, you should raise them more often.)

So, if you are in a game where people frequently limp (for the bring-in), you often should limp in behind them, especially if the players are weak. What you are usually hoping is to catch a perfect card on fourth street, and thus you must be prepared to fold if you don't catch what you want. (Remember, you need to avoid making any compounding errors.)

Here's an example. If you are holding

and the queens and tens are live, you should frequently call the bring-in. Also consider the kings, jacks, and nines.

If you should catch a king or jack, that's great. If however, you catch a queen or ten on fourth street (giving you a gut shot) your decision is not automatic. How long you stay with the hand will depend on whether you have seen any of your other straight cards, as well as the other kings, jacks, and nines; how much money is in the pot; what you think you must beat; and how you think the hand will be played.

(By the way, how the hand will be played is a hidden factor and is extremely important. It gives you an idea of how much you can win if you make your hand and what it will cost you if you don't. This is a concept that usually is considered only by very advanced players.)

Calling for the bring-in allows you to punish people who don't raise enough. For example, if two or three people are in and you have a hand like

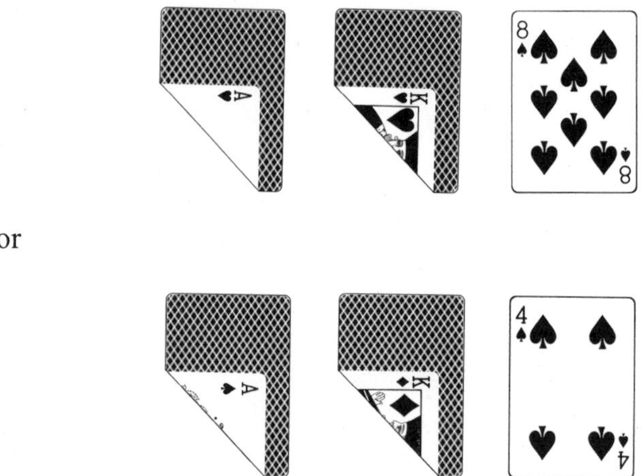

you should call if your cards are live.

This is an especially good play against a player who will pay you off all the way if you make your hand. However, notice that in the examples above you had a two-flush. If this was not the case you probably wouldn't want to play against three players (including the bring-in).

As already mentioned, you must take into account whether your hand has the potential to improve enough that it would be a mistake for your opponent to pay off all the way. Here's an example. Suppose you start with:

If you catch a nine, your opponent probably is correct to call all the way with just one pair because you are holding a hand that can easily be beaten. Thus, this hand is barely worth a call, even for a bring-in against typical opposition. However, against players who will pay you off all the way if you make open fives, then it becomes worthwhile to call.

Finally, remember that these ideas apply mainly to only calling the bring-in. If it is a full bet, it wouldn't hurt to abstain from calling with weak hands. (The exception is when you were forced in with the low card. See "Part Three: Miscellaneous Topics" — "Defending Against the Possible Ante Steal" on page 101.)

Playing Extra Hands Heads-Up

Earlier we mentioned that you want to play as many profitable extra hands as possible. Many of these occur in heads-up situations. Let's talk about some of them.

If you can get heads-up with someone who plays badly, plays too loose, can be easily manipulated, or you can read easily, then you should play many hands against him. Let's see why this is so.

Suppose you are in an eight-handed \$30-\$60 game. If we don't count the bet on the river you will be risking \$180 to win \$230 assuming that there is a bet on every street.[4] But if you find yourself against someone who does not always bet every round, you may be risking as little as \$120 to win that \$230. So against this person (in a heads-up situation), you should play many hands that might not normally be worth it, especially if he can be manipulated.

Here's an example. A player with an eight raises, you have

and think that he only has a pair of eights. First, notice that there are many cards that you can catch that will scare him. This includes all cards above an eight. In addition, you know that one of his eights is out. If no one else is in and you are in a late position, you can play this hand. If it comes out badly on the next

---

[4] Unless you are against a very tricky player, the bet on the end usually, but not always, favors the drawing hand.

card, for example, you catch a trey and he catches a suited nine, you should fold. But if it comes out good, you can become the aggressor. However, you need to be heads-up. If someone else has called his third street raise, you should throw this hand away.

Heads-Up Versus Multiway

Let's talk a little more about heads-up versus multiway. The main thing to remember is that as the number of players increases certain hands go down in value. For example, suppose you have:

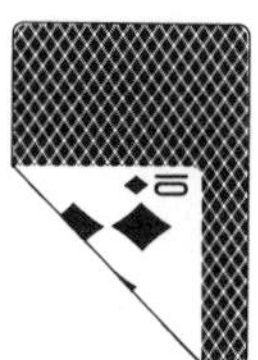
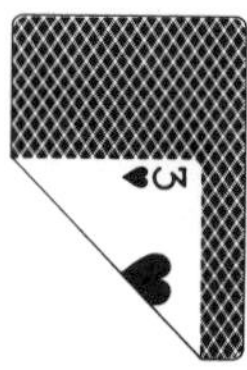

In a loose wild game, this is not a good hand. In fact, this hand usually should be thrown away (in this type of game), unless the two tens are in the hole.

As should be obvious from our previous discussions, big pairs are better heads-up, while drawing hands are better multiway. This means that you should raise or reraise with big pairs, unless your raise or reraise is unlikely to thin out the field. As we have already explained, if a jack raises, everyone calls, and you are last with

it may be better to just call and see what develops. A problem with reraising in this situation is that you make the pot so large that your opponents who otherwise would play badly by calling from fourth street on are now playing correctly. Also, not reraising disguises your hand so that it is easier to thin out the field later. In addition, it introduces an element of randomization to your play.

Of course, there is an exception to this, and it is an important one. You still should raise for value if your hand is extremely strong and completely live. For instance, in the example just given, you have a suited ace instead of the four as a kicker and none of your cards are dead, you probably should go ahead and make a big pot.

Another factor to consider is that there is a good chance you will lead on the next round because of your large upcard. This is a reason to consider raising since it is less likely you will be able to thin out the field on fourth street. If the kings were hidden, calling would be correct. (Of course, if first to act and one of your kings is up, you can check and then raise if a bet comes from a late position player.)

If you have a big pair and only a small number of people are in, you should just about always raise (or reraise). Sometimes you should reraise even with a small pair in a multiway pot. Here's an example. Suppose you are low with:

Five people call your bring-in, and then a jack raises. You usually should reraise. The reason for this is that your reraise is a better play than either calling or folding. First, you most likely will knock out everyone but the jack. Second, the pot is large enough that folding is wrong. And, as we have stressed, the hand plays better heads-up against a probable pair of jacks, especially with all that "dead" money in there contributed by the other callers.

Even if you are 100 percent sure that the raiser has a pair of jacks, you still should reraise. And unless your opponent pairs jacks on board, you should be prepared to go to the river.

Third Street Afterthought

As we stated in the introduction to this section, play on third street in seven-card stud is quite complicated. Thus, even though we have examined a great deal of material, situations occasionally arise that we did not cover. But if you study what we have written you should understand the general concepts and therefore be able to handle just about any difficulty that occurs.

Remember that the most important decision you will make in seven-card stud is whether to play your hand. Mistakes made on third street can quickly compound themselves and become quite costly. Also, keep in mind that some hands play better heads-up, while others play better multiway. In fact, as the text shows, some hands that should be played heads-up for a raise or reraise should be thrown away if you have several opponents. Conversely, some hands that should be played multiway should be folded if you believe the pot will probably be heads-up.

Finally, the most difficult third-street strategy to master is that relating to small and medium pairs. As stated previously, these hands are significantly worse than big pairs. Don't automatically play small or medium pairs. And, unless you are on a steal, make sure that they are live when you do play them. If you follow the guidelines, these hands can be played for substantial profit. Otherwise, they can become quite costly.

Part Two

The Later Streets

The Later Streets

Introduction

Even though we have stated that the most important decision you will make in seven-card stud is on third street, this does not mean that the later streets are unimportant. In fact, just the opposite is true. A great deal of money can either be won or lost by making correct plays or committing errors *after* the decision to participate in the pot has been made.

One of the things we shall see is that how you play your hand frequently depends on how you think your opponent will play his hand and how he will react to you. In seven-card stud the pots often become very large compared to the size of the bets. This means that if your opponent is easy to manipulate — that is, you have good control over him — you gain a significant advantage. On the other hand, if you can't manipulate your opponent, your task becomes much more difficult.

In addition, we will see that in many situations it is important to raise to get the pot heads-up if possible, and thus give yourself a maximum chance to win. This is true even if the cards you are holding may be second best. There are also many situations where it is correct to quickly throw a hand away. Getting your opponent to call in these spots can be quite profitable.

We already have seen that correct seven-card stud strategy on the first three cards is quite complicated. We now will see that this complexity continues through all the streets, in spite of the fact that large pots sometimes force even expert players to play like everyone else.

Fourth Street

If you think you have the best hand on fourth street you usually should try to eliminate players. For instance, suppose after receiving your second upcard you have what you believe is the best hand, are first to act in a three-person pot, think the second player is weak, and are sure that the third player will bet. Your play is now to try for a check-raise.

Here's an example. Suppose you limped in with

are called by the 7♣, and are raised by the Q♠ (meaning a probable pair of queens). If you happen to catch a king on the next round, and your two opponents catch seemingly non-threatening cards, you should try for a check-raise if the probable pair of queens is last to act. However, if the queens will act directly after you, it may be best to bet, hoping that the queen will raise, which should eliminate the third player from the pot.

However, trying for the check-raise is sometimes wrong. This could be true if you raised coming in on third street or if you catch a scare card on fourth street. Your threatening board may cause the last player to check.

Another thing to keep in mind when trying to make this play is that the opponent on the end needs to be an aggressive player. Don't check to someone who might be afraid to bet because of your initial raise or because of the overcard or scare card you may have just caught.

It is also important to try to add deception to big pair play on fourth street. For example, suppose you have two aces and your board is ace baby. By betting, you are telling your opponent that you most likely have a big pair (unless your opponent's board is weak, in which case your bet becomes somewhat automatic).

If you check in this situation and your opponent bets, you should occasionally flat-call. However, it is usually best to raise. A raise not only will get more money into the pot immediately, but also may psychologically commit your opponent to go all the way, even if you catch cards that indicate he should get out. The main problem with just calling is that you will be first to act on fifth street, and if you check again, your opponent may now check behind you, saving a bet and giving himself a free card.

Now suppose you have a fairly good hand and your opponent catches a suited card that goes well with his medium upcard. If you are high, consider checking. By checking, there is a good chance that your opponent will bet. He either has a good draw or is likely to represent one.

Here's an example. You have:

Your opponent started with

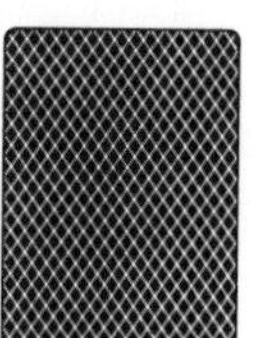
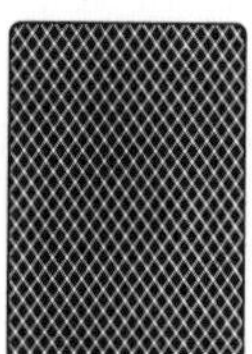

and catches the

You usually should check and call. If you check, the money almost always will be put into the pot anyway.

If a good player calls on third street against a possible steal raise and it is then checked to him on fourth street, he usually will bet. This means that if you raise in a steal position on third street with, let's say, a king up, are called, then catch a complete blank on fourth street, and your opponent catches something even mildly scary, you almost always should check, whether you have a hand or not. Furthermore, you should usually not raise as the better play is to wait and see what develops.

Unlike Texas hold 'em, where you can steal fairly often on the flop, you cannot steal a lot on fourth street in seven-card stud. If someone *calls* on third street, he usually doesn't fold on the next card. (Distinguish this from the player who *raises* on third street to steal and then folds on fourth street when he is caught.)

Now suppose you have a hand like:

 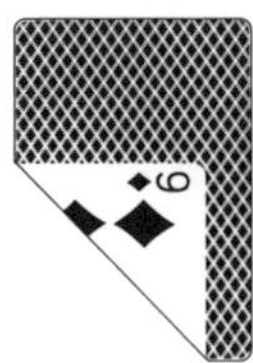  

You usually should throw your hand away if you are facing a bet from something like ace-queen suited. This would be correct even if your kickers were better. The only hands that you should call with are those holdings that can improve to very large hands, specifically hands that can beat aces up. Playing hands like the one illustrated is a common fourth-street error, and can be very costly.

Realize that if your opponent catches an ace on fourth street, he has caught a dangerous card. This is because many players call with high cards or with a small pair and an ace kicker — especially if there was no raise on third street — and even if your opponent hasn't paired his ace, he may pair it down the road. So when someone catches an ace and bets into you, be cautious. (See "Part Three: Miscellaneous Topics" — "Throwing Fast Balls" on page 124.)

Pairing Your Door Card on Fourth Street

When you pair your door card on fourth street, you can make either a single or a maximum bet (or check). For example, in the \$15-\$30 game, you would have the choice of betting either \$15 or \$30. Most professional players automatically will bet the maximum, or occasionally check. But there are three distinct situations when you pair your door card (on fourth street) where making the single bet is correct.

Suppose you have made three-of-a-kind or a higher two pair than your opponent can have. For example, you pair sevens and have kings in the hole, while he shows jack-five offsuit. This probably is one of those times when you should bet the minimum.

These times occur when you are quite sure that a maximum bet will cause your opponent to fold, but you don't want him to fold even for half a bet. Put another way, if your opponent will make a mistake by calling you for half a bet, why not make that bet instead of a maximum bet that will force him to (correctly) throw his hand away.

Even if you are not heads-up, this single bet may still be correct. Any time you are sure that your opponents will fold for a full bet, and you do not want them to fold even for half a bet, you should consider betting the minimum instead of the maximum. This play typically comes up against weak players, particularly tourists, who can't resist a bargain.

However, when you make trips, you should not always bet the minimum. If you become known as someone who often makes this play, observant opponents will realize that when you bet the maximum, you probably don't have three-of-a-kind. In a multiway pot, if you think there is a chance that someone will call the maximum (and you have made trips), then bet the maximum, even if his upcards look weak. (Keep in mind that in a multiway pot, your opponents are getting better odds, so you really don't mind winning immediately.)

Another time that you usually should make half a bet is when you have only one pair and are convinced that if you are beaten you will be called for either a big bet or a small bet, and if you are not, your opponent will fold for either a big bet or a small bet. In addition, the more observant players might fold even when you are beaten, since you also are sometimes betting the lesser amount when you have made trips.

Here's an example. Suppose a weak player showing the 3♦ brings it in. You start off with

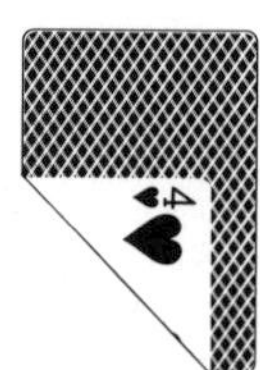

and just call. Everyone else folds. Your opponent catches an offsuit queen, and you make open sevens. You should bet the minimum, not the maximum.

The reason the minimum bet is correct in this example is that if your opponent has queens, he will call for either the minimum or the maximum, but if he does not have queens, he should fold for just a single bet. So why gamble the extra money? If you bet the minimum and your opponent does call, then you should assume that he has queens.

The third time to bet just the minimum is when you don't have much, and you think you are beat and will be called if you bet. However, you also believe that if you check, your opponent will bet the maximum and you would consider calling his bet. This situation won't come up as often as the two just discussed; nevertheless, it is still important.

Here's an example. Suppose you call with

are raised by a jack, and are fairly sure that you are up against a pair of jacks. Now you make open sevens. Since you would like to see another card you would rather get called for half a bet then check and have to call a double bet. Of course, if you think your opponent will fold, you should bet the maximum. But this is usually not likely. Many players automatically will call if they have a big pair or a big draw. However, for the minimum bet to be correct, your opponent must be likely to bet the maximum if you check. If you think he won't bet but will call if you bet, your best play is probably to check.

But suppose in the example just given that instead of the 2♥, you have an overcard, such as the K♥. You now should bet the maximum. This is because you have more outs if you are called.

If you make two small pair, (while pairing your door card) either multiway or heads-up, you always should bet the maximum unless you decide not to bet at all. The time to check two small pair is when you are planning to fold if the other person bets. An example would be when a tight player raised with a small card showing and pairs his door card. Since he probably has two higher pair you should check and fold.

Even though most opponents will get suspicious when you pair on fourth street and check, there are situations where you make trips and should check. These are the rare cases where it seems quite likely that you have only one pair.

Here's an obvious example. You are low with:

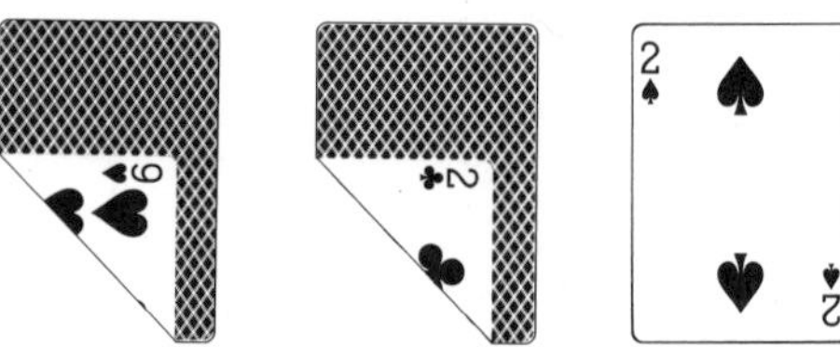

Nobody raises. Now you pair your door card, giving you trips. If the last deuce is out, and you are against four or five other people, you probably should check. Notice that you would certainly check if you had only two deuces.

Another thing to realize in this situation is that your hand (trips) might not be very strong, especially if some of your opponents have caught dangerous cards. But you still would rather check-raise than bet right out. It is usually a mistake to wait until fifth or sixth street to raise. You should raise immediately on fourth street, because just calling tends to give your hand away anyway. So you may miss a later opportunity. Also, another benefit of check-raising early is that it may make an opponent fold, which means that he won't get a fifth-street card to beat you.

Finally, suppose you make four-of-a-kind on fourth street. No matter how obvious it is, you should check. The standard advice is to check against terrible players, but to bet against good players because they won't be fooled. However, this is probably wrong. Even good players don't have the psychological strength to fold a full house against one pair showing on fifth street, even if they are almost sure they are against quads.

Here's an example. A bunch of small cards call the bring-in, you have

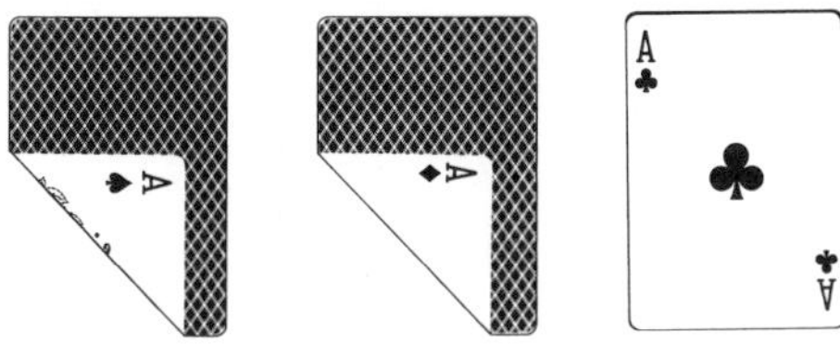

and you raise. On fourth street, you catch the A♥ and your opponents catch nothing special. You should check.

If you bet on fourth street, anyone with two pair will fold. If no one catches anything good on fifth street, you probably should check again. You may even want to check all the way through to the river if their boards look weak, in the hopes that someone makes a flush or a full house and pays it off. Very few players are capable of folding hands this strong, especially if no one has made a bet throughout the hand. (We hope this is a problem you will have to deal with many times in your poker career.)

Fifth Street

The decision on fifth street is a close second in importance to the decision on third street. This is because fifth street is when the bets double in size and a call usually ties you on to the end, which may mean putting in an additional two or more large bets, especially in an aggressive game.

Suppose you have a hand, such as a flush draw, that you will at least call a bet. Instead of checking, you should bet this hand if some reasonable chance exists that your opponent will fold. An example is if your opponent has caught two blanks, and from the way the hand has been played, you suspect that he started with a three-flush or a small pair.

However, there are times when you should check. These times occur when you know your opponent will always check behind you — and you want this — and you are absolutely certain you will be called if you bet. However, even under these circumstances, it may be better to bet to set up a steal on a subsequent round.

A common misconception is that you want to keep as many players in as possible on fifth street if you have a drawing hand. This is not necessarily true. If your drawing hand can make a big pair that might win against one opponent, you may want to raise. (Or if you already have a pair, you may want to raise to limit the pot to two players.) A raise on fifth street also may get you a free card.

A similar concept is that if you have a choice between playing against either one or two opponents, it is often better to be heads-up, because you may win with a bigger pair or two small pair. Moreover, in a two-person pot, your opponent may not bet if you catch a big card.

It is also correct to raise on fifth street with a drawing hand if many players are in, you are in a late position, and you think you have the *best* drawing hand. You need to be fairly sure that your hand has the best potential. Remember, your opponents can have big cards that you don't see and thus may be drawing to a bigger straight or flush than you.

On fifth street, it is important to eliminate players when you believe you have the best hand. In other words, almost never give a free card.

However, if you are against many opponents and only have one big pair you should usually check, even if it seems like you have the best hand. This is because there is a good chance that everyone will call, and you will be a bigger dog than the number of bets that you are collecting, because of all the different combinations that can be out. If you have the worse hand you are in bad shape if someone raises you. If you check and everyone checks, you usually give up very little. (But it may be correct to check-raise if you can knock players out.)

Another fifth street concept is to recognize those times you should raise when you are almost certain that you do *not* have the best hand.

Here's an example. A player who has just caught an offsuit ace checks. The next player has

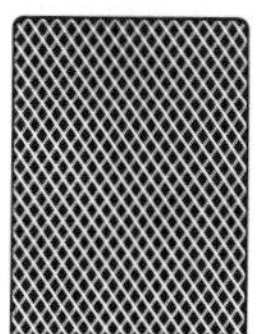 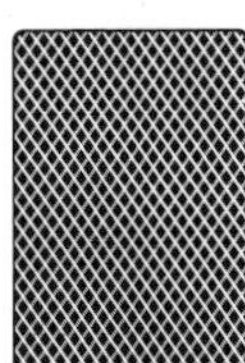   

and bets. You have two queens and a three-flush, and your cards are live. It is a multiway pot. There is a person behind you who you suspect has two kings, and you think the bettor started with a pair of tens and probably has made two pair. The correct play is to raise to drive out the other hands. This play notably increases your chances of winning (though you are still a small underdog) because you now are much more likely to win if you improve your hand.

This is a very important concept. Failure to raise in this situation will cost you significant money in the long run. Another advantage to this raise, besides possibly knocking out the other players, is that it might gain you a free card on sixth street. In the situation just described, you should bet on sixth street if you improve; otherwise, it is usually best to check.

However, raising in similar spots on fifth street is not always correct. Suppose an opponent makes an open pair (but doesn't pair his door card). He bets, meaning a probable two pair. If you are next to act and have one higher pair, you might raise to try to eliminate the other players. But this is not the same situation as described earlier. Sometimes your opponent will have trips. For instance, he may have started with a three-flush and paired on fourth street.

In general, trying for a check-raise on fifth street is not good strategy since your check may cause you to lose a double-size bet. You need to be very sure that your opponent will bet. Also, your check may allow a miracle card to beat you.

If you pair your door card, it usually will stop your opponent from betting. This means that it is almost certainly wrong to try for a check-raise in this spot. The time to attempt a check-raise on fifth street is with concealed trips or sometimes a high two pair. However, if your fifth-street card is the same suit as your door card, but you actually have hidden trips, you usually should bet and try to represent a flush draw. You definitely would not try for a check-raise on fifth street against weak timid players, because they do not bet often enough.

Occasionally there are other benefits to a check-raise on fifth street besides getting more money in the pot. For instance, a check-raise might get you a free card. The play is to represent a strong hand in such a manner that if you miss on sixth street, your opponent will not bet (after you check).

Here's an example. You raise on third street with

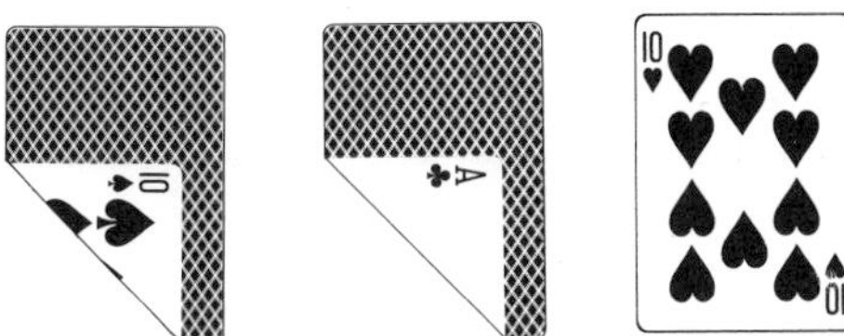

and are raised by a queen, meaning at least a pair of queens. On fourth street, you both catch blanks. He bets and you call. On fifth street, you catch a king versus another blank for your opponent. Check-raise a weak player. (Notice that you have two overcards plus a pair.)

On sixth street, if you catch an ace, you will get an extra bet. If you catch a king, your opponent will fold, which you won't like, but at least you got more money in the pot. And if you pair your fourth-street card, your opponent probably will fold, and you want him to do so. Another advantage to check-raising in this spot is that your opponent may fold immediately, especially if he has been representing two queens but actually has less.

If you have a small pair and a three-flush on fifth street and someone bets, neither calling nor folding is automatic. When deciding whether to call, you must consider what you think you have to beat, how much money is in the pot, and how the hand most likely will be played from that point on. If most of these are favorable, you should call.

Usually call on fifth street with a small pair if you have either an ace or two overcards to your opponent's probable pair, and if your cards are live. Automatically folding in this situation (which a lot of players do) is very costly. In other words, it is worth chasing a larger pair in a heads-up pot on fifth street if you have two live kickers higher than your opponent's probable pair or a live ace kicker. But this assumes that the pot is offering you approximately 4-to-1 odds at this point, and that there is no reason to believe your opponent has more than one pair.

Here's an example. On fifth street you have

and your opponent has

He has represented a pair of kings, and has been betting all the way. You should call him on fifth street as long as your hand is live.

Sixth Street

Sometimes on sixth street you find yourself in a situation where you are either a small favorite or a huge underdog, but you don't know which. When this happens, it is best to check and call. An example is when you have a big pair and are probably against a smaller pair, but you could also be against a flush.

If you do bet on sixth street, you will be called. Even weak hands almost always will stay with you, unless your board is extremely scary. But they probably will bet in these spots if you check, so you get the same amount of money in the pot without risking a raise. (By the way, your opponents are playing correctly when they call on sixth street, because the pot usually is so large that it becomes correct to chase.)

A common sixth street mistake is not raising when a raise may knock out a third player who might beat you. Failing to raise can cost you the pot by allowing a weak hand to get good enough pot odds to call and outdraw you.

You can try for a check-raise on sixth street when you are fairly sure you have the best hand and are against an aggressive player who likes to bet medium and big pairs. Your check-raise also may make your opponent throw his hand away (although this is an unlikely event).

Here's an example. Suppose you have a hidden high two pair or hidden trips, but your first two cards were suited. You bet on fourth and fifth streets, but have caught apparent blanks on fifth and sixth streets. Against an aggressive opponent, who you believe has a good pair and will put you on a four-flush, you can try for a check-raise. (But if you are against a timid player who might not bet, trying to check-raise would be wrong.)

The opportunity to occasionally make an even more creative play (against tough aggressive players only) occurs when you have paired your door card on fourth street and have made trips. If your opponent has called your fourth- and fifth-street bets, he doesn't think you have three-of-a-kind, and you therefore can check-raise on sixth street.

If you are not sure about trying for a check-raise, it is best to go ahead and bet. There are two reasons for this. First, you may lose a bet by checking, and second, there might be some chance that your opponent will fold, which means that he can't get a free card to beat you.

Another supposedly "expert" sixth-street play is raising to get a free card. For example, suppose you have been betting all the way with a big pair, but now your opponent makes a small open pair and bets into you on sixth street. If you think his best hand is two pair, and you have a good draw to go along with your big pair, you might raise. If you improve on the river, bet after your opponent checks; otherwise, just show the hand down.

However, even though this play is fairly common, there are logical problems with it. Unless you have something to go along with your pair, such as a flush draw, you are an underdog to improve. This means that you don't save money by raising without a draw. The strategy is correct only if there is a small chance that your pair is the best hand. For example, suppose you have a big pair against a probable smaller two pair. If you don't improve, you have cost yourself a bet if your opponent would have checked on the river. Also, you may run into trips (or better) and get reraised.

There is not that much to say about play on sixth street. And the fact is there is not that much play to it. This is because the pot usually has become too big at this point to allow you to profitably fold, even if you know you are beaten. So except for sometimes making or saving an extra bet or getting out when drawing dead, the expert generally plays sixth street just like everyone else.

Seventh Street

Suppose that going into seventh street you have an obvious pair of aces, and your opponent has an obvious pair of kings. If you improve down the river, your options are to bet, to try for a check-raise, or to check with the intention of calling if your opponent bets. If you don't improve, your options are to bet, hoping that one pair will call; to check with the intention of calling, hoping to catch a steal; to check with the intention of raising, hoping to make two pair fold; or to check with the intention of folding.

Betting either a pair of aces or aces up, hoping that one pair will call is usually the best play when your opponent's cards are slightly dead. Automatically betting aces up and checking a pair of aces (as many people do) is not correct.

If you think your opponent will call 100 percent of the time when he does not improve, then the correct play is to bet both aces and aces up (and three aces). Many players consistently lose money by not taking advantage of this bet.

On the other hand, if you think your opponent will always bet if he has made kings up or three kings, then you should check, unless he almost always will call with just two kings. This is because you don't lose anything when he has kings up and you have aces up.

If you think your opponent usually will check two kings (and sometimes fold if you bet), but will bet kings up or better — and, assuming that he does bet, call if you check-raise — then you should check aces with the intention of folding and check aces up with the intention of raising. However, if you think he will bet only kings up or better but *fold* kings up if you check-raise, then your correct strategy is to now check and call with aces up, (since he might have three kings), but to check-raise with two aces to make him fold kings up!

When making this last play, another thing to consider is that a typical player is more likely to fold a hand like jacks up rather than kings up. (Notice that if you find an opponent who plays like this, you can't lose unless he makes trips on the end. If you don't improve your aces, you win a showdown when he doesn't improve and steal the pot by check-raising when he makes two pair.)

Suppose you have made two pair on the end, such as queens up, your opponent bets, and he has been representing a pair of kings all along. Normally this is an automatic call. However, you probably should fold against a very timid and readable opponent who never bets one pair for value when all the cards are out. On the other hand, against a very aggressive player who almost always will bet kings for value, it may be correct to raise with queens up. If your opponent's upcards are dead *and* you think he will call your raise with just one pair (or might fold a higher two pair), you can profitably make this play.

When you have made a big two pair, one thing to consider when determining whether to bet is how concealed your hand is. It makes a difference whether your big pair or your small pair is showing. For example, if you have kings over fours, you would prefer that neither pair is showing, especially the kings.

As can be seen, seventh street should be played imaginatively. Those of you who play automatically on the river and don't consider who you are against, plus the other factors just mentioned, are making a big mistake.

One thing to keep in mind on seventh street is that most players will call if you bet, and also will call if you raise or check-raise. This means that raising on the end as a bluff should be done only rarely.

However, raising as a bluff may be correct against an opponent who will bet a mediocre hand for value on the end, but who also is willing to throw his hand away if raised. Another time is in a three-way pot to knock out the winner. Notice that your raise in a three-way pot is not exactly a bluff, since you still need a better hand than the initial bettor.

If you are caught raising on the end without a hand, it might be correct to try it again if your opponent thinks you won't do it more than once. But make sure you know your opponent well.

It is rarely correct to lay down a decent hand on the end for one last bet with a large amount of money at stake. However, if you know a player extremely well, you can make some laydowns that normally would be wrong. But your judgement must be accurate.

It is sometimes possible to get three bets on the end against an aggressive player. For example, suppose you have made a full house and believe your opponent has been trying for a flush. If he makes his hand and you bet, you can then reraise after he raises. In addition, your opponent may miss his flush but still make something, such as a high pair, and call. On the other hand, if your opponent is the timid type, it is probably better to try for a check-raise to win two bets.

To reiterate, you usually should call on seventh street because the pots get so big. However, if you face the threat of a raise from a third player, it might be correct to throw your hand away. Still, remember, the biggest mistake you can make mathematically is to throw away the best hand when the pot is large.

Calling on the end with a hand you should not have called with can never be a big mistake. The most it can cost you is a bet, while not calling can cost you the pot. Another reason to call is to prevent players from bluffing you in the future.

Suppose your opponent, who has been high all the way and has been checking to you, suddenly bets on the river. You should never fold (unless you have absolutely nothing) if this player has shown that he will bluff in this situation. Another time you should call a "surprise" bet is when it appears that you may have been bluffing up to that point.

Here's an example. Suppose you start with two aces, one of which is up, and another ace is out. If your opponent catches the case ace on fifth or sixth street and bets into you on the river, he may be bluffing since he will think you don't have what you are representing.

It should be noted that not betting for value on the end can't be a big mistake since you have cost yourself mathematically only a fraction of a bet. But these fractions add up. And not raising when you should raise can be a disaster if it allows a third player to overcall and beat you. But heads-up, you again are costing yourself only a fraction of a bet when you miss a raise, therefore it is not so terrible. On the other hand, if you are fairly sure that your raise will be called by a worse hand, you eventually will cost yourself a lot of money by not raising in these spots.

When your opponent has a pair on board (not involving his door card) and he bets, raising him if you have made a straight or a flush is an option you should consider. It depends on your opponent. If it looks as though you have a four-flush and you are still bet into, you could have a problem. However, a good player often will bet when he is looking at a possible straight or flush draw if he thinks it is likely for you to have only a pair. But if a weak or scared player bets, be more concerned.

Finally, you occasionally can bluff on seventh street, especially when you have a four-flush showing, but have absolutely nothing and are pretty sure that your opponent is trying for a higher flush. You also can sometimes bluff if your opponent has a pair showing. If the pair does not involve his door card, you can bet at a player who is capable of laying down two pair. With one pair on board, your bet will likely convince him that you can beat at least two pair. Somewhat surprisingly, this bluff works better if your opponent's on-board pair is big, particularly if you raised on sixth street.

The Later Streets

Afterthought

As we have seen, appropriate strategy for seven-card stud beyond third street is quite complicated. You must be able to evaluate your hand, taking into account how live your cards are, whether your hand contains any scare cards, the action that has taken place so far, and how your hand compares with your opponents' board.

Speaking of opponents, how you perceive them and how they perceive you is very important. For instance, as the text has pointed out, different players react differently to any scare cards that you might catch. Terrible opponents virtually will ignore them, while great players will have a good "feel" for when they are truly dangerous and when they are more likely to be harmless.

Another thing to keep in mind is that the later streets do not play themselves. This is especially true on seventh street. Automatically checking, betting, or raising is never correct. Always consider alternatives. Here again, accurately evaluating your hands — and your opponents — will help ensure that you make the best decisions. Finally, even though in seven-card stud the majority of money is won or lost on third street, the advanced player who is an expert from fourth street on probably can win as much as 50 percent more than someone who plays well on third street, but just average after that. Yes, play on the later streets is quite important in this game. Get good at it.

Part Three

Miscellaneous Topics

Miscellaneous Topics

Introduction

So far, we have discussed a lot of different topics. Yet in seven-card stud, there seems to be an infinite number of unique situations and possibilities that can occur. In this section, we will address some of these miscellaneous topics, plus try to clarify some concepts and ideas already covered.

Some of the ideas we have thus far presented have never before been correctly discussed in print. This also applies to much of what follows. In fact, since so little has been written on seven-card stud, a great deal of this material is probably quite new to a lot of readers. Many concepts are not easy, but once they are mastered , you will be able to consider yourself an expert player — that is, once you also have acquired the experience necessary to achieve success in this difficult game.

Also, keep in mind how many of these concepts seem to interact with other concepts and ideas we have been discussing. One of the keys to successful seven-card stud is the ability to understand exactly the situation you are in. For example, having a live hand can be tremendously different from having a hand that is semi-dead.

Finally, we would like to remind you that it is much easier to comprehend the underlying concepts of seven-card stud if you have read *The Theory of Poker* by David Sklansky.

Defending Against the Possible Ante Steal

As we have seen, ante stealing in seven-card stud is an important part of winning play. This means that most of your opponents also will be attempting at least some steals and that you must be able to defend against them.

This is especially true in the bigger games, as the ante and bring-in are proportionately larger compared to the bets and the players tend to be more aggressive than those at the smaller stakes. This is also true in tight games. In loose games, players call with many hands, thereby making it unlikely that someone will try to steal the antes. Let's get into some specifics.

Suppose a late-position player raises and you think he might not have much. What should you do? If you think this player will frequently fold a lot of his hands, you can reraise with virtually anything. Unfortunately, there are not many players who play this way.

If you think your opponent has little but will call your raise, one option is to just call and bet into him on fourth street if you fall high and he catches bad. (If he catches good, be prepared to fold if your hand is weak.) When making this play, you need to be fairly sure that your opponent is the type of player who will fold on fourth street if he is weak. Though more players will fold on fourth than will fold immediately for a reraise on third street, many of your opponents automatically will go to fifth street.

Now suppose that your opponent, who you think is likely to be on a steal, has a larger upcard than you do, and you have next to nothing. The correct play usually is to fold, unless you are fairly sure that you can maneuver your opponent as just described. The reason for folding is that even if your opponent is weak, almost all players will call your reraise hoping either to pair their upcard or to catch some other card that improves their hand or at least looks scary. Furthermore, they probably will find a reason to continue playing their hand if you bet on fourth street. Thus, you usually still need to have some sort of a decent hand to reraise a possible ante steal.

If you have a small pair and a weak upcard, and you are last to act, you should call against someone who is on a likely steal. Remember, most stealers will call a reraise if you have a small card showing. Consequently, it is usually best to wait until at least fourth street to try to take the pot away from them.

If your pair is a little larger, you can consider reraising against a possible steal. In fact, you probably should reraise about half the time (with your better hands) in this situation. One thing to consider is the rank of your opponents' upcard. The lower it is, the more inclined to reraise you should be. For example, against an ace, rarely reraise; against an eight, reraise much more often. (This is because your opponent is less likely to raise back, since you might have a higher pair in the hole.)

If you are the bring-in, and your opponent who has raised from a late position does not have an ace or a king up, you can call if you have two big cards (higher than his upcard) in the hole. If you catch a scare card, or an ace or a king, and your opponent "rags off," then you can bet and often take it. However, when your upcard is very low, it may be better to just throw your hand away, as even your opponent's steal hands may be too strong for you and there are less scare cards you can catch.

Here's an example. Suppose you have

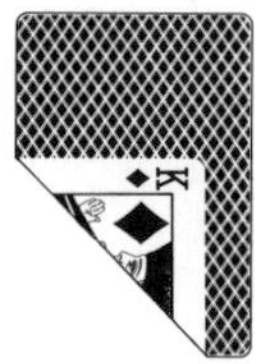

a player in a steal position with a 9♣ up raises, no one else is yet in the pot, and you know that he will raise with anything. You normally can go ahead and call. If your opponent's upcard is a queen or higher, however, you should fold. You also might fold with a smaller upcard.

If, however, you feel that your opponent requires some sort of hand — perhaps he will only raise with 50 percent of the hands dealt to him — then this call is too loose.

Playing Two Pair Against a Hidden Big Pair

Earlier in the text, we stated that if you raise on third street with a small or medium pair and are reraised by an obvious big pair *in the hole,* you should call. The reason for continuing with the hand (besides your pot odds, of course) is that except for the last card, your opponent cannot make two pair without you knowing it.

If your opponent makes two pair on fourth, fifth, or sixth street, you see it and thus save money since you throw your hand away. Had your opponent instead reraised with a big card up, you usually would not know if (or when) he makes two pair.

If you know your opponent has a big pair in the hole, you should call all the way to the end, as long as he hasn't paired his board. If you make two hidden pair, you should raise (or check-raise) but usually not until sixth street. The reason you should wait until sixth street to raise is that no matter when you raise, your opponent will not fold his big pair. You will be able to get only one raise in, so you may as well wait to make sure that your opponent does not draw out on you. For instance, if you raise on fourth street and your opponent makes an open pair on fifth street, you will wish you had not done it.

However, there are times when it is correct to raise before the sixth card. One time is when your board develops "kind of scary," such as a three-straight or three-flush on fifth street. Another time is against a timid opponent who might check on sixth street, even though he would have no reason to believe that his pair of kings or aces is not the best hand. But the general concept is that if an opponent is betting into you, and you figure that your hand is better and you have only one chance for a raise, you should wait until sixth street to get this raise in.

Here's an example. You start with

and catch the

on fourth street. Your opponent catches a blank and bets it. It is almost always correct to wait until sixth street to raise if you think you are facing a hidden big pair. However, if you caught the 8♥ on fourth street, your board now shows two straight flush cards and is beginning to develop in such a way that you may want to get the raise in before sixth street. But keep in mind that if you raise and then make an open pair that fills you up, your earlier raise is likely to cause your opponent to fold, and you don't want him to fold.

(It is important to understand that waiting until sixth street to raise only applies to heads-up situations. If the pot is multiway, you should try to run out as many opponents as possible as soon as possible. This means to raise immediately or perhaps to try for a check-raise.)

Suppose you have paired your door card on fourth street and have two small pair. The correct play is to bet the maximum into your opponent and hope he throws his hand away. If he calls, continue to bet unless you have a good reason not to, such as your opponent makes an open pair. Remember, if he knew what your hole cards were (meaning that he knows you do not have three-of-a-kind), it would probably be correct for him to call you all the way.

Playing Against a Paired Door Card (on the Early Rounds)

If your opponent pairs his door card, you should fold most of the time. This is particularly true on fourth or fifth street when the pot is not yet too large. The most important exception is when your opponent is a wild, loose player who plays almost any three cards, plus you can beat his pair.

There are other exceptions as well. The first is when the low card brought it in, did not have to call a raise, and now pairs his door card. The second is when a lower card raised earlier, you are very sure he has a big pair in the hole, and you have a hand that either:

1. Can beat his likely two pair.
2. Contains a higher pair than what you think he has in the hole, and the pot is large. Or,
3. Is a live four-card draw.

You can also play if you doubt that you are up against trips and you have two bigger pair than your opponent's open pair, such as nines and eights versus sevens showing. It is much better for both of your pairs to be higher than his open pair so that if he does have trips and fills up, your potential full house will always beat him.

If someone with a low card, who was not the bring-in but who called a raise on third street, pairs his door card, you usually should fold. For example, if someone limps in with a seven up, calls a raise, and catches a seven, you usually should throw your hand away unless you have a straight flush draw or can beat three sevens.

Again, if you have any doubt about what you should do when your opponent pairs his door card on fourth street you should fold. (If someone pairs his door card on a later street, be more inclined to call, but only because the pot is now bigger.)

One time that you should be more inclined to call is if one of your opponent's trip cards is dead. But don't use this concept as an excuse to *usually call*.

Here's an example. Suppose on third street your opponent has

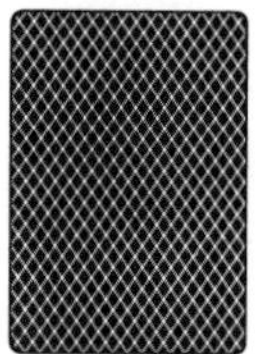  

and there were three other clubs out. Now it is more likely that he has trips if he pairs his door card. However, if no clubs were out, he is more likely to have started with a flush draw. If no clubs were out *and* a seven was dead, you would be inclined to continue playing even if he makes open sevens on fourth street.

If your opponent is a weak player who had the second highest upcard and did not enter the pot with a raise, he may be less likely to have three-of-a-kind if he pairs his door card. This would be particularly true if he was the first one to voluntarily enter the pot and the player who holds the highest card acts after him. The reason for this is that many players are reluctant to raise in this situation unless they have a pair. They will always call with a three-flush or a three-straight being afraid of the high card still to act behind them. However, not all players are like this so you must be sure that your opinion is correct.

To summarize, if your opponent pairs his door card early you should usually fold, unless you have good reason to believe that you are not against three-of-a-kind and your hand can stand a lot of pressure. Specifically, one big pair usually should be thrown away (on fourth and fifth streets), especially if one of your pair cards is dead.

(Expert players understand that the reason for this caution is not just the fact that you frequently are up against trips or two high pair. First of all, one high pair is not much of a favorite against one smaller pair and a three-flush, which is another likely hand your opponent could have. Second, the subsequent bets put the high pair at a further disadvantage, as the door-card pair can decide whether to continue betting or not. See the section on "Effective Odds and Reverse Effective Odds" in *The Theory of Poker* by David Sklansky.)

Continuing with a Draw

When you play a three-flush, if you catch a fourth suited card on fourth street, you usually should be prepared to go all the way. However, if you don't catch a suited card on fourth street, contrary to what many players think, you still should call about 60 percent of the time.

This 60 percent comes from the fact that you should call if you have any kind of improvement or if other conditions are favorable. Specifically, call if you have made a small pair, if your cards are live, if your cards are high, if you have straight possibilities, or if you are getting big odds. For instance, with a small three-flush, if you catch an offsuit king, you usually should call because you now may be able to win the pot by pairing kings. Of course, if you think you are against a pair of aces, you should fold. You also should fold on fourth street, even if you make a small pair (with your three-flush), when you are absolutely sure it will cost you a double bet or if you think you are up against more than one pair.

In general, you need a good reason not to call with a three-flush on fourth street. This might be when your cards are out or the card that you catch is absolutely of no help. Many people who think they are playing well fold too many three-flushes on fourth street. The idea that you usually need to catch a suited card to continue playing is simply wrong.

If you do make a four-flush on fourth street, the correct play is usually to either bet or raise and be prepared to see the river card. However, there are times when you would abandon a four-flush before the river card. The most obvious is when one of your opponents makes something extremely threatening, like two pair or three-of-a-kind on board. Another time you should abandon a four-flush, and very few players know to do this, is when one of your opponents pairs his door card and his play strongly indicates trips. However, if the pot is extremely large, it is correct to call.

If you happen to make a large pair on fourth street or beyond to go along with your draw, the pair is now the main consideration to your strategy. That is, try to eliminate opponents where appropriate, and play heads-up against a smaller pair if possible.

Much of what is appropriate for flush draws also applies to straight draws. For instance, if you make a four-straight (open at both ends), you want to play to the river unless one of your opponents makes something extremely threatening on board. (This now includes a four-flush.) But if you don't improve to a four-straight, how long you stay with the hand depends on what you think you have to beat, how much money is in the pot, and how the hand will be played from that point on. In general, you use much the same criteria as you do for staying with a three-flush but you should be less likely to call if you catch a blank than you would be if you started with a three-flush.

If you make a four-straight, how you should play depends on the situation. Sometimes call, but sometimes raise. Experience, as well as many of the ideas discussed in this text, will help you make the proper decision.

If you start with a three-straight and on fourth street make a small pair or an inside straight draw, you should still throw the hand away if you think you may be put in the middle and the pot is small. The time to play in this spot is when there are bigger cards in your straight draw (to pair) than what you might be up against and it will cost only one bet. However, if you catch a complete blank, you should usually pass even if your three-card-straight contains overcards.

Playing a Big Pair Against a Possible Flush or Straight

Sometimes it is best to check and call with a big pair on fifth or sixth street. This would be correct if you find yourself against a three-flush showing or a hand like:

The reason this check is correct is that first, most opponents automatically will bet with this type of board. And second, if you bet and are raised, you usually should call anyway. Thus, by checking, you get money in the pot when you have the best hand, but you save money those times when your opponent is very strong.

If you are facing a three-straight or three-flush and have a two hidden pair or trips, you still should check. Then you normally would call with the two pair and check-raise with the trips (unless you are almost positive your opponent has a made hand.)

If your two pair or trips include a pair on board, be more inclined to bet into his threatening board, as he will be more inclined to check behind you (if you check) rather than represent a hand he doesn't have.

Playing Big Cards Against a Medium Pair

Suppose on third street, you have a hand like

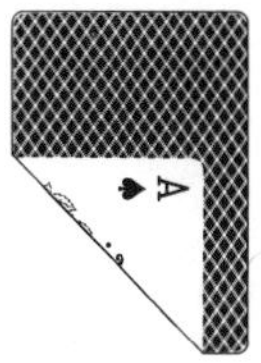

and a medium upcard such as an eight raises, meaning that you are against a likely medium pair. The correct play is to reraise if there is no more than one high card behind you and your hand is live. Otherwise fold.

The reason for raising is that you would prefer to play heads-up. This is particularly true if you are against an opponent who does not require a big kicker to raise.

On fourth street, if you catch bad and your opponent catches a scare card, you should check and perhaps fold. But if both you and your opponent catch bad, you usually should bet. This allows you to set up a steal on fifth street, assuming that your opponent calls your bet on fourth street (as he probably will).

The time to attempt a steal on fifth street is when your opponent catches a second blank. For example, if your opponent's board is something like

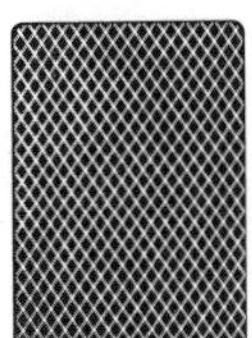

you should bet no matter what you may have. It is especially nice if you pair your fourth street card, as this almost guarantees stealing the pot with the worse hand.

Scare Card Strategy

If you hold a weak hand, an important consideration in determining whether to bet is if you can get your opponent to fold on the next round if you catch a scare card. Here's an example. On third street, you raise with

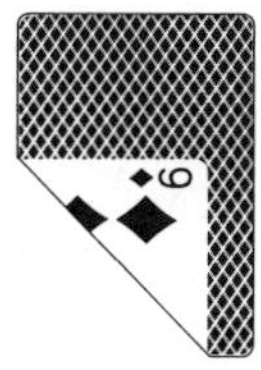

and are called. You catch the suited A♠. You bet again and are called. (This worries you, because you have a pretty strong board.) You still should bet one more time if the next card is any spade, if it pairs your board, or if it is any other card such as an eight or nine that improves your hand.

In other words, if your hand is worth a call or even almost worth a call if your opponent bets, it is better to bet yourself (even if there is no chance that your opponent will fold) if your bet may allow you to steal on the next round. This might occur if you then happen to catch a dangerous card, such as a pair or a suited card, that makes your opponent think you are more of a favorite than you really are.

Even if you started good, catching a scare card still should help your hand. Unless you have a monster, you don't mind the fact that a threatening card may win the pot for you immediately.

Although your bet will not always make your opponent more likely to fold on the next round, it is still sometimes worthwhile to bet, because in these situations you make more money when your bet is called.

Here's an example. Suppose you have

and you think your opponent has a straight draw or perhaps something like a pair of sixes. You should still bet, though he might fold on the next round even if you check on this round. The reason for betting is that many cards you can catch will make you more money when your opponent initially calls and then folds, or calls and then gets beat. Notice that the cards which will help you to win the pot, either eventually or on the next round, are any deuce, eight, or nine, as well as any spade. Also possibly an ace, a seven, or a ten.

However, if you catch a scare card, you should not always bet into a good aggressive player or a great player, because great players fear scary boards less than (reasonably) good players (but more than bad players).

Next, let's suppose on fourth street that you have a medium pair, a person in front of you bets, and a player behind you catches a scare card. You usually should throw your hand away. Here's an example. Suppose you are second in a three-way pot and start with

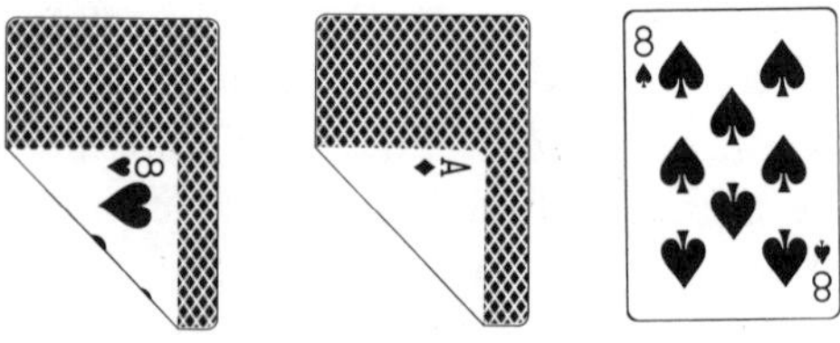

and now catch a jack. A queen bets after catching a king, and the player behind you has caught a card that gives him two straight flush cards on board. Unless the pot is very large, throw your hand away immediately!

Buying the Free Card on Fourth Street

There is a standard play on fourth street that almost all the good players make — and so should you. Against weak players, if someone bets on fourth street and you have any kind of scary board whatsoever, you should raise and then give yourself a free card on fifth street after he "checks to the raiser." This play is especially correct when your hand is likely to bet last on the following round. Also keep in mind that this play works better if the fifth street cards that would make you first (to act) on that round would be good for you.

Here's an example. Your opponent has

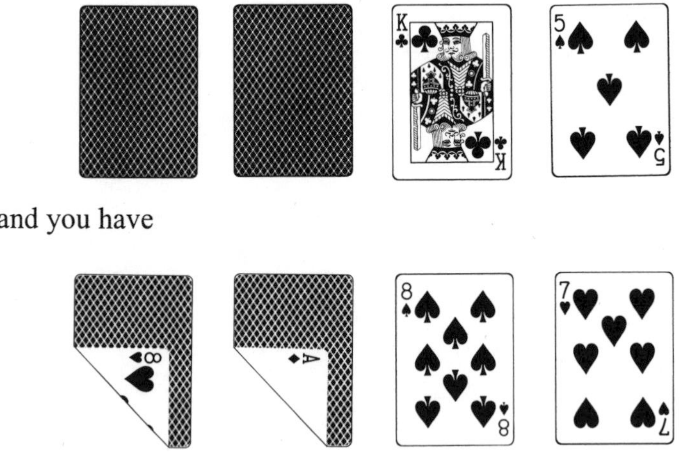

and you have

You should raise (as long as your opponent is a weak player), even if you are positive that you are against a pair of kings. Notice that the only cards you can catch to make you go first on the next round are cards that improve your hand.

After making this play, if your opponent checks to you on fifth street, you do not always have to check if you don't improve. An alternative strategy is to bet on fifth street and take a free card on sixth street when appropriate.

However, against a very good player, you should often not make this play. This is because you might be reraised or just called and then bet into on the next round.

Suppose you started with:

Your opponent, whose door card is a face card, catches a non-threatening card on fourth street and bets. You can now raise, especially if your fourth-street card appears to go well with your door card and/or you now have a three-flush.

Another example. You have

and your opponent started with a king up and caught a baby on fourth street. Raise if he bets. Notice that if you catch an ace or a king, making you high, you have improved your hand since you now have straight potential.

Here's a more risky example. Your opponent has

and you have

Notice that a raise in this spot has some drawbacks, since a queen, a king, or an ace will not help you very much but may force you to bet first. However, you still should make this raise against weak opponents because they are so likely to check to you on the next round. But if you now catch a high card and have to go first, you cannot get a free card, unless your opponent is so timid that your raise on the previous round makes him afraid to bet even after you check.

Unfortunately, you will not be the only one who makes this type of play. It is routine for good players. The best counter strategy is to call your opponent's raise on fourth street, and then go ahead and lead on fifth street when his card does not seem to help him and you think he was trying for a free card.

However, you might get raised again! If this happens, you should still probably call. Remember, in seven-card stud, you are almost never drawing that slim.

Buying the Free Card on Fifth Street

There is a similar play to the one in the previous section that can be used on fifth street. If your opponent bets on fifth street and you have a hand that you plan to call with on both fifth and sixth streets, you might want to raise on fifth street. You would tend to do this when you are quite sure that your opponent will check to you on sixth street if you make this play. Now you can take a free card. This play is especially worthwhile if the card you catch on sixth street scares him out (incorrectly). This play is even better if it is also true that the card that really does help you on sixth street does not scare him.

Here's an example. Suppose you have

and your opponent bets an apparent pair of jacks. You should raise, especially if you are almost certain that your raise will get your opponent to check on sixth street. (However, if he still will bet into you on sixth street, you don't really mind since your hand is almost as good as his.) Check it right back if you catch a blank. If you catch a heart, you bet, and your opponent should call (making you extra money), and if you pair the six or the four, your opponent likely will fold and you want him to. Also, bet again on sixth street if you catch an ace, a king, or a queen, and be prepared to bet on the river as a bluff.

Your opponent often will fold when you pair, because he will be afraid that he is drawing dead. But when you catch a heart, your fifth-street raise will make him think your hand is anything but a flush (unless he is an expert who knows this play also.)

An Expert Play

Suppose a good player with a strong upcard raises on third street and you call. On fourth street, he catches "good" and you catch seemingly weak. He bets and you call. On fifth street, he again catches a strong card and you again catch what looks like a possible blank, and this time he checks. You usually should bet and expect to take the pot.

Here's an example. Your opponent starts with an ace up, catches a king, and then catches a nine. You start with a jack up, catch a seven, and then are dealt a six. Bet on fifth street if your opponent checks after betting on the previous two rounds.

The reason this works is that your opponent has decided not to semi-bluff anymore and hopes instead he can represent a slowplay. Then, when you bet, your bet shows him that you must be strong. The idea is that when a good player checks what appears to be an obvious betting hand on fifth street, you often can steal the pot.

Sometimes you can set up this play. For example, suppose someone with the last high card up raises in a late position and no one else has yet called. If you have a small pair or perhaps two high cards in the hole, you can call. If he bets on fourth street and you have not improved, go ahead and call, unless he has caught something extremely threatening. On fifth street, if he checks, bet and take the pot.

Throwing Fast Balls

Sometimes situations will develop on fourth or fifth street where you're betting with what appears to be the best hand that has the potential to cost you a great deal of money. Here's an example.

Suppose you start with:

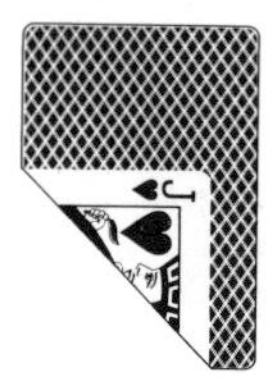
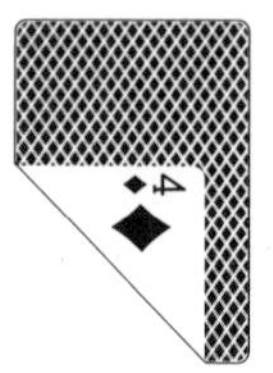

You raise and are called by a player whose upcard is lower than yours. As far as you know he could have a pair or perhaps a three-flush. Now on fourth street he catches an ace and you catch an inconsequential card. That ace creates a problem for you since it might have hit his hand.

Typical players will bet on fourth street after their opponent checks, and again on fifth street. However, if they are now against a hand like aces up, they will be check-raised on fifth street, and will frequently continue with little chance.

But suppose you play your hand differently. When he catches the ace on fourth street and checks, you check behind him. Let's see what happens.

You start off with J♥4♦J♣ and catch the

On fourth street your opponent is showing:

He checks and you check behind him with the pair of jacks. What's going to happen here?

On fifth street, (with the above boards) your opponent will usually bet. If he has aces up you will save a bet and a half. If he has a pair with an ace you have cost yourself a small fraction of a bet by not betting on fourth street. And if he has nothing, you have extracted money from him. However, you shouldn't check on fourth street if you catch a card that goes well with your door card.

It's important to understand that in stud, the better board should be in command. But if your opponent wants to relinquish that right, it's often better to take a free card. Don't throw too many fast balls.

Quick Notes
(On a Variety of Subjects)

If you have a small pair with a big kicker and are chasing an opponent who holds a probable larger pair (but smaller than your kicker), you should throw your hand away if your opponent makes an open pair on board (not his door card) and the pot is not too large, unless you have improved your hand in other ways (such as picking up a draw or another overcard kicker). You now have fewer outs since you most likely cannot win if you make two small pair. This usually means that you should fold in this situation on fifth street, but often call if his pair doesn't show until sixth street. You also would like to have seen one of his open pair cards already out to reduce your chances of running into a full house.

Here's an example. Suppose you start with:

You are against a probable pair of jacks who makes an open pair of deuces, and you have caught all blanks. You should fold on fifth street, but go ahead and call if he doesn't pair until sixth street, especially if you can account for one other deuce.

Suppose on third street, with a small card up, you make it two bets, suggesting that you have a probable big pair in the hole. Now if you catch an open pair on board and your opponent calls (no matter what the street), you are probably against some sort of draw since he is calling to continue facing what looks like two higher pair.

If you have a gut-shot draw to an ace-high straight on fourth street, you still usually want to play the hand to the end. But you also may prefer to play the hand heads-up, hoping to win with a big pair. For example, suppose on fourth street that you hold

and are against several players. Your best strategy may be to raise a bettor on your immediate right or to try for a check-raise.

Any time a tight player calls from an early position with a small card up, and there are several big cards behind him, his most likely hand is a three-flush (unless two or more of that suit is out elsewhere).

One time that you should fold is when you are sure that you are against a big pair in the hole, and your opponent has caught all possible cards that could give him three-of-a-kind. For example, suppose on third street you raise with

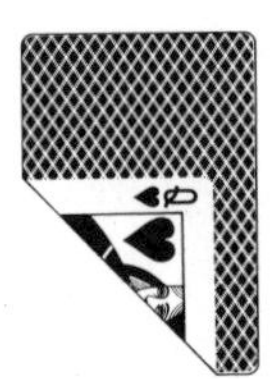

and are reraised by someone holding a small card, and you know you must be against a bigger pair. If this opponent now catches both an ace and a king, you should throw your hand away, unless you have picked up a draw.

Miscellaneous Topics

Afterthought

One point that we have emphasized repeatedly is that seven-card stud is an extremely complicated game. This is easily seen by all the topics covered in this section alone. In fact, it is probably fair to say that no book on seven-card stud can cover everything, simply because there are so many possible situations, and individual play is quite diverse.

The most significant error that typical players make is to call when someone has paired their door card. The section that discusses this concept is extremely important. Remember, if you are in doubt, *throw your hand away!*

Also keep in mind to avoid playing similar hands the same way all the time. Some variation is needed to throw the better players off. However, as we have pointed out, a lot of deception is not needed against the weaker players. Against this type of opponent, solid play is usually best and will get the money. And remember, those hands that are the best candidates for deceptive plays are the ones where you do not give up much when you check instead of bet.

Also, a lot of the fancier strategies that we have discussed are correct only when the situation and/or conditions are right. Don't fall into the trap of making a lot of great plays just to make great plays. You should be trying to win the most money, not to impress everyone at the table.

Part Four

Playing in Loose Games

Playing in Loose Games

Introduction

Since the original edition of this book in 1989, both poker and seven-card stud have undergone an explosion. Today there are many new players participating, resulting in much looser games, especially on the East Coast. It is not uncommon, even at the higher limits, to find many players who not only play too many hands, but go too far with their hands.

Needless to say, for the skilled player these games are very profitable. But they do require significant adjustments and many otherwise winning players do not do a good job in this area. In addition, we have yet to see any advice that is totally accurate on how to play in loose games, even though much has been written.

This being the case, we have added an expanded "Playing in Loose Games" section to this 21st Century Edition of *Seven-Card Stud for Advanced Players.* We suggest that you read it many times. It contains some ideas that are quite sophisticated and very different from what you may have previously read. We also know that this advice in the appropriate game can be highly profitable.

An Important Point

Before we delve into strategy, we want to stress a point that is very important in these types of games. When you are playing against bad players, the idea is to make the maximum profit from their mistakes. This is very different from playing perfectly.

For instance, theoretically you could program a computer to play expertly with proper game theory tactics and randomization so that, heads-up, nobody could beat it. However, that same program would not beat a bad player out of as much as is possible because it would be assuming the other guy is playing well.

Now, there is almost no question that if your opponent plays badly, and you continue to play *assuming* he plays well, you will still win. But you will not win as much as someone who is adjusting to his poor play. And that is why most good players underperform in very good games. They do not adjust enough to optimize the amount of extra profit that can be made when someone is playing badly.

Here's just one example of what we are talking about that doesn't involve specific strategy. When you are against bad players it is probably detrimental to *mull* over your decisions. When you sit there and think, you encourage bad players to play better against you.

You must understand that someone who plays poorly may do so for a variety of reasons. He might be an idiot. He might be drunk. Or he might be there to have fun. And it is not fun to play proper poker. It's too boring — you don't play enough hands.

In many locations you constantly run into people who know how to play pretty well if they have to, but don't. In a tournament they tend to play a little better, but their overall play is poor because they are there to have a good time. Of course they enjoy winning more than losing, but they enjoy playing most of all.

Now suppose that one of these players sees you debating over a decision. Believe it or not, some of them are *unwittingly* turned into better players against you because they begin to realize that there is more to this game than just having fun. We have noticed this over the years, and it usually occurs when a "fun" player sees a guy thinking hard about a particular decision.

So let's say that you are in a game like this, you bet, and someone raises. Decide whether you are going to fold or call *quickly*. Don't give that person, or others at the table, the opportunity to realize that you do in fact *think* about decisions. What may happen if you don't follow this advice is that the "fun" player tightens up against you, but also thinks "You know what, I think I'm going to try to bluff this guy. I don't think I could against someone else, but maybe I'll throw a raise in against him. I don't know if I have the best hand, but he thinks about throwing away so many hands, who knows."

Notice that you accidentally make them play closer to the proper strategy. When a weak player sees you sitting there and thinking, you may cause him to play better, especially against *you*.

If you suffer from this problem, here are some suggestions. Since you only spend extra time on hands that are close anyway, you should quickly do one thing or another at random. Since the decision is close, neither one can be that bad. Better yet, every time you would stop to think, just call instead. It's better than thinking.

Another way to get around this problem is to be ready for every situation. Think one step ahead.

An obvious example would be when you flop top pair when there is a two-flush on board. If the flush card gets there on the turn and you bet, know ahead of time whether you will call or fold if your opponent raises.

We have a friend who is a very good player, but who exhibits a characteristic that we don't like. When he bets with a good hand he will fold quickly if someone raises him (if he thinks that folding is the correct play). That is good. But he also does the converse, which we disagree with. That is, when he is bluffing and gets raised he thinks for awhile. The reason he does that is that he doesn't want to make it obvious that he is bluffing. So even though he knows that he is never going to call, he still thinks.

Our contention is that against bad players you shouldn't think in this spot either. You shouldn't care whether the guy thought you were bluffing or not. What is more important is that you don't want to portray that you are capable of throwing away good hands for one more bet and that you look at every single decision critically. That can become a disaster when someone unbeknownst to you picks up on it, and steals the pot from you for one extra bet. It is terrible to create an atmosphere where someone whom you have noticed never bluffs will try a bluff only against you. Again, the reason why he tried it against you and not anybody else is the ambiance that you portrayed that has registered in his mind.

You must attempt to display a carefree attitude in your decision making. (However, you don't have to be "everybody's pal" or the "life of the party.") In this way it will be unlikely for the stranger to pick up on you as being one of these guys who "I think I can run a bluff against." (So you continue to throw your hand away when he does show strength.)

Besides stopping bluffs, another reason to act less seriously and in an apparently unthinking manner is to keep everyone relaxed and "playing loose." A serious thinking mode of play on your part will not only cause people to make plays against you, but will also often make them tighten up. Players don't want to feel like suckers who are helping this serious pro make a living.

There are other things you should do or not do along these same lines. For instance, you should never make a play that makes a fool of a person. There will be times when a check-raise is clearly your best option. But if it is heads-up and you are against one of these "weakies" who is there for the fun of it, don't do it.

Now we don't pass on this play because we are afraid that it will make him quit. Rather it is because if you make a fool of a guy (with a check-raise for instance in a heads-up spot), he is going to tighten up against you and focus in on you for the rest of the game. He is no longer there to have fun. He is there to beat you. He is now playing better. You have put him in a frame of mind other than "let's just be here and have a good time." (It is okay to check-raise in multiway pots since no one is likely to take this personally.)

Besides not thinking or acting seriously or using tricky heads-up plays, there are other things you should not do if you want people to play badly. For example, throwing cards or getting mad when you lose a pot. You never want the tourist to say to himself "I'm here to enjoy myself and have comradery with everybody. If I beat this guy he's going to be so upset that it's not going to be fun anymore. I don't want to have to feel guilty when I win."

So these are some non-strategic concepts which are important to know in order to keep bad players playing badly. By this we mean "weak-loose." That is, they are playing too many hands, they are not doing very much bluffing, they are easy to read, and they are going too far with their hands. That's the ultimate for you.

An Important Concept
(Borrowed from Razz)

There is an important concept involving loose games and bad players that is best illustrated by a situation in the game of razz. For those of you who don't know, razz is seven-card stud played for low. The game is explained in detail in the book *Sklansky on Poker.*

One concept that Sklansky addresses, which we will expand on here, is that if you hold a *slightly* better starting hand than your opponent you shouldn't reraise their opening raise if that opponent is a bad player.

Here's why. Suppose you start with a three card 6 and your opponent raises with a seven up indicating a probable three card 7. The problem with reraising him is that when there is a double bet on third street it becomes proper to take a second card on fourth street regardless of what happens. If there wasn't a double bet on third street, it would be proper to fold on fourth street if you catch a big one and he catches a baby. But your opponent won't make this fold if it comes the other way. So you should just call to keep fourth street from becoming a "shootout" where you and he will now play the same.

The general idea is that you extract the most money from your opponents by putting them in a position to make big mistakes. Sometimes that means manipulating the pot size into one that is most likely to be a size where they make errors. Occasionally you make the pot bigger early to make them chase more those times you flop a great hand. Other times you keep it smaller to keep the hand from being a shootout where you have to chase just as they will. Of course, it is not worth making these plays if you give up too much on the earlier round. Only in marginal situations should you make a lesser expected value play for the sake of future benefits. But these marginal situations do come up a lot, so try to recognize them.

Returning to Stud

So, how do you apply the previous concepts to a very good seven-card stud game? That is, in a loose, passive game where many people play on third street and then play poorly after that you should:

1. Play more hands than you would if the players were better, especially if you can get in for just the bring-in. This is because weaker hands are still often better than theirs and also because even if they aren't you can often outplay them later on.

2. Often try to keep the early betting down to the size of the bring-in or just one full bet on third street. This is because you gain a lot when bad players make incorrect calls on fourth street and beyond, as long as the pot is kept small.

Let's discuss this second point in a little more detail. Even if you have a good hand, you should be a little less apt to raise than if you were against better players. This is not only because the hand doesn't do well against many people, but for a second reason: With a hand that is *pretty* good but not great, if you don't raise (and thereby cost yourself a *little* bit of money at that point), you gain it back *plus* some because had you made the pot bigger there would be less opportunities for your opponents to make significant mistakes later on.

Here is a general example. Suppose you know that a raise with a particular starting hand gains you $3 in expectation. It could still be wrong to raise. The problem is that by putting extra money in early you may make your opponent's play on fourth street and beyond become "accidentally" correct or close to it. This might cost you more than the small amount gained on third street. Thus, while you should *play* more hands than almost all pros do, a lot of those hands that seem like automatic raises should not be raised. You want your skill to mean more on further rounds.

There is a bit of a two-edged sword here. If you're playing against extremely terrible opponents, it's hard not to raise with pretty good hands because even though you're costing yourself money on the later streets, you're gaining so much on third street since your hand is usually so much better than theirs. In other words, if people are coming in with absolutely everything, you have got to raise with a pair of jacks simply because your hand is so much better on average than so many of the other players.

But if these players are playing merely a bit looser than what they normally should, and then they play meekly and badly, a good reason not to raise is that when you make the pot larger, you are now making some of your opponents play correctly. This is in addition to the fact that some of these hands, such as the pair of jacks just mentioned, don't do well in multiway pots.

There is also another reason why you want to play a few more hands in these loose, good games: It is the fact that since you're playing a lot of hands, even if these extra hands don't show much long term profit, your opponents will see this. Thus when you do have a top quality hand they won't throw their hands away as much because they are frequently seeing you in the pot.

When there are many people in the pot certain hands go up in value. They are basically the three-flushes, as well as certain high three-card-straights, even the ones that have gaps in them. For instance, a hand like

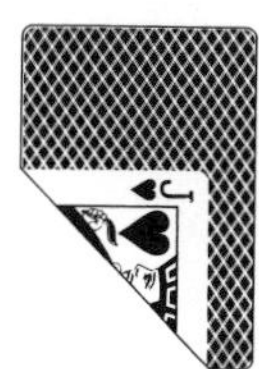

becomes fairly good because of the two-flush in addition to the straight cards if all of your cards are live. We have discussed this before in other parts of the book, but this concept is even more important in these loose games.

(By the way, when we talk about playing certain hands in loose games, we mean because the pot is multiway or you expect more people to call behind you. But even loose games sometimes have only heads-up pots, and therefore, you adjust your strategy and play your hand as you would in a short-handed situation. The fact that the game in general is loose doesn't mean that you also change your strategy for those times when the pot is short-handed.)

The Horse Race Concept

One key concept that should always be understood about loose stud games is the *horse race paradox* that was discussed in *Getting the Best of It* by David Sklansky. That is, if you have a horse that runs a good, steady time; or a poker hand that is good, but cannot improve, you run into a mathematical paradox. For instance, if this hand has a 60 percent chance of surviving against a drawing hand, that is the drawing hand has a 40 percent chance of beating you, it's only a nice situation to be in when you are against only one such drawing hand. However, if you are up against two such drawing hands, though you are getting 2-to-1 odds, your chances have dropped down from 60 percent to 60 x 60 percent, which is 36 percent. All of a sudden you would barely have the best of it.

Against three drawing hands, each of which has a 40 percent chance of beating you, your chances of beating all three go down to 21.6 percent. Since you are getting only 3-to-1 odds, you actually have the *worst* of the four hands. (Remember, this assumes that your hand cannot improve to beat those hands when they do make what they are drawing for. If you in fact could "draw back" on them, it would totally change things.) Notice that this has some serious implications for multiway poker pots.

In a nutshell, the idea is that if your hand is only fairly good, without too much chance of improving to a very strong hand, the more players drawing against you, the worse it is for you. A straight on fifth street against many flush draws is one example. A more common example would be a high pair on third or fourth street against many players. What this means as far as your strategy is concerned in seven-card stud is this: If your hand is simply good, but not great, it is important to try to thin the field down to one or two opponents. This is fairly easy to do in a tougher game; however, it's not so easy if the game is loose or wild.

When you are in such a game you must reverse strategies. Tough games require early raises to thin the field, but early raises in loose games just cause you extra trouble with these mediocre hands. The better strategy is to put in as little money as possible early on with some of these questionable hands. The idea is that since you are often going to be folding on fourth or fifth street, why commit too much money to the pot?

There is the second reason as well. It is that keeping the pot small early on may allow you to thin the field out on the next round. This is because:

1. If you do not raise with some of your merely good hands on third street, it is more likely that someone will *bet into you* on fourth street, allowing you to raise and now cut down the field.

2. The fact that the pot has been kept small means that it is more likely that other players will fold since they have so little invested.

An example of this type of play would be if you have

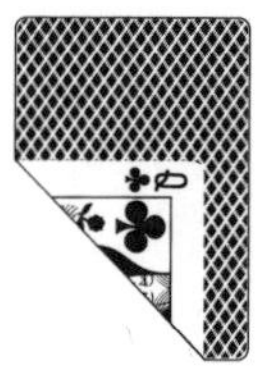  

and another queen is out. A deuce brings it in, a seven calls, and a nine calls. It is probably right to just call, and then be ready to raise or check-raise on fourth street if no one catches a threatening card. On the other hand, if people do catch threatening cards and you catch nothing, you should just throw your hand away right there. For instance, if the seven catches an ace and comes out betting, your hand should be folded. Even if the six catches a suited five, you should be ready to fold your hand if it doesn't improve and the pot is small.

So the idea is to merely call on third street, and to play from that point on (if someone bets) only under one of three conditions:

1. You improve on fourth street.
2. Everybody catches non-threatening cards.
3. You have the opportunity to get the hand heads-up.

If none of these conditions materialize, be very inclined to fold on fourth street, and certainly fold on fifth street if you still have not improved, or cannot get it heads-up.

This concept should not be taken too far, however. Remember, the idea is that you play this way if your hand cannot easily improve to a very strong hand. If, for instance, you have

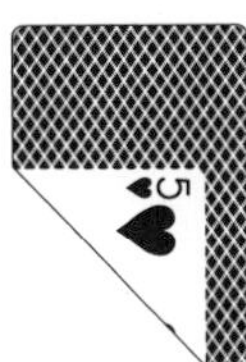
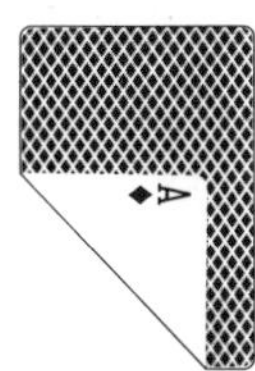

you should raise or reraise, even in a multiway pot as long as all the aces and fives, and most of the hearts, were live. There is just too good a chance that you're going to make a hand that will be able to survive the onslaught of many players. The same would be true for a hand like:

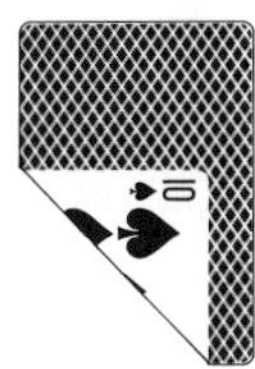

Again, in this case, it is not necessary to keep the pot small so that you can get it heads-up later. You have a good chance of winning if everyone stays in.

Getting High Implied Odds

It makes a big difference if you can get in for merely the bring-in with a hand like

This is because you are looking to catch perfect and take advantage of the high implied odds that getting in cheaply will provide. So when the game is good, you should play more hands, such as one gap three-straights, but only if it appears that you can get in cheaply with them.

The trap that you *don't* want to get into is calling with hands that won't make enough profitable situations. So you throw away a hand like

 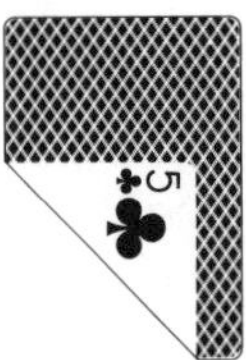 

particularly if your hand is not live. (You might play if a nine was dead and the situation was very favorable, but it can just about never be correct if a five is already out.)

On the other hand, if you are in a loose, passive game where they usually call, but only occasionally raise, you should play any pair with a two-flush. You should also be playing a hand like

under the gun, and anything better. You should play these hands because you are going to win a lot when you hit them. That is, you take advantage of their bad play. Conversely, you often shouldn't raise with your medium pairs and sometimes not even with your high pairs in spots where you would raise in tougher, tighter games.

When the Pots Get Big

When the pots get big, tricky situations are created on the later streets. This should dominate your approach to playing a hand. Basically your number one priority is to win the pot. Not to win more money. However, winning the pot is not that simple. It isn't just a matter of thinking "I have the best hand, therefore I bet." It might be better to check in order to get someone in late position to bet so that you can check-raise. It might be better to bet hoping someone else will raise. And it might be better to set this up on the previous round.

For instance, suppose you have two aces and are high on board with an ace up. You raise in an early position and get several callers. On fourth street you are still high and no one has caught anything threatening. Our preferred way to play this hand is to check and frequently only call if the bet comes from a player on your left. A check-raise here will not eliminate anyone. All it will do is to make the pot bigger where you have several players drawing to beat you. However, if the bet comes from your right you should usually check-raise in an attempt to knock people out.

For example, you start in early position with:

You raise and get four callers. On fourth street you catch the

and no one else catches anything threatening. If you bet they are all going to call and are usually correct to do so even if their initial call was wrong. Thus it is usually best to check and hope that a bet comes from your right so that you can raise.

It's so important to increase your chances to win the pot that it can be right to bet or raise with a hand that you know is beat. For instance, if on fourth street you have

a player on your right who has just caught an ace checks, and you strongly suspect that the player on your immediate left has a pair of queens, it is almost mandatory to bet (hoping that the player on your left will raise). You do this not only because you might make a flush, but because it is important to get other hands out so that you can increase the chance that you will win if you make a pair of kings (or small two pair).

This is something that very few players are aware of. In other words, your bet adds some possible ways of winning because when you bet and get raised, hands like small pairs and many hands that contain an ace will fold. The general concept is that if you have an overcard to the likely big pair and would continue playing for one bet you should frequently bet yourself in order to entice a raise from the likely best hand and get the pot heads-up.

Likewise, you yourself should often raise a likely high pair with a similar hand if he bets.

This play is similar to the idea that we discussed earlier in this text when we pointed out that it is important to get heads-up if it significantly improves the chances that you can win the pot. (See "Part One: Third Street" — "The Number of Players in the Pot" on page 16.)

This means a lot when the pot is big. The point is that when many bets are in the center of the table you don't worry about saving bets. You do everything possible to maximize your chances of winning.

Sometimes it can get extreme. For instance, if the pot is really large, you might play a hand strangely and seemingly miss bets or raises.

Suppose on fourth street the player on your right bets, you have a larger hidden pair (than either of his upcards) but you know that if you raise four or five players will come in behind you anyway. If the pot is big you should often just call. Now when the player on your right bets again on fifth street, you can raise and thus force those players who are drawing to beat you, to call two double size bets.

Here's a specific example. You have

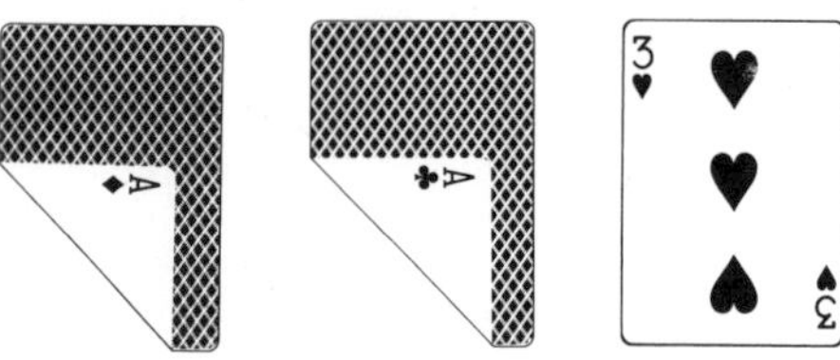

you are the bring-in, there are five people in for a raise and a reraise, and the reraise was done by the player on your immediate right who has a king up indicating a probable pair of kings. You raise again in an attempt to knock some players out, but everyone calls. On fourth street no one catches anything to indicate that your hand is not still the best.

Now this may sound insane, but if the player on your right (with the probable pair of kings) bets, rather than raise right there, you should often just call and go for the raise on fifth street because *that* raise will knock people out. The raise on fourth street won't.

Now it's true that when you just call on fourth street someone will often make two pair or pick up a draw that eventually beats you. But that's just the point. They were going to call even if you raised and because of the size of the pot they are right to do so. In addition, had you raised and then bet on fifth street, they would call again, and once again be correct.

However, if you play the hand as we suggest, while they can still make two pair to beat you on fifth street, they may not have the opportunity to make two pair on sixth street or the river. Thus you at least keep them from drawing out on the last two cards.

The general idea is that this type of play may be correct when no one is going to fold for the bet or the bet and raise on fourth street, but you think that a raise can knock them out on fifth street. But it is not foolproof. The danger is that occasionally someone who would have folded now beats you. Another drawback is that you don't collect those fourth street bets when your hand does hold up. But as the pot gets bigger and bigger the pros to this play usually outweigh the cons.

Just to recap a bit, the most important thing in these very large pots is to play your hand in such a way that no one will draw out on you on the end (or to give yourself the maximum chance to win if you miss your draw but happen to make a big pair). That one edge more than makes up for any missed bets. By playing in an unorthodox way you can sometimes get players out who would have beaten you on sixth street or the river card because you have managed to cost them two double size bets on fifth street. That is worth giving up a lot of other small profits.

It's Important to Have Other Outs

If your big pair also contains a two-flush (or your three-flush also contains a two-straight) it's a *giant* advantage in loose games. One of the nice things about raising with a big pair and a two-flush on third street is that if you catch two more suited cards you welcome all smaller pairs calling on fifth street. They may be right to call if you only had the big pair, but the four-flush will give you more ways to beat them. Now you want them to call.

Thus, one of the reasons to raise on third street with a pair and a two-flush is because you might pick up a draw in addition to your pair. By your making the pot bigger, people now play hands that can't win against your hand if you hit the flush.

Let's be specific. Suppose you hold:

If several players in front of you have just called, you should raise (unless your hand is dead) if you are in a game where the players are fairly weak. However if they are tough you should just call.

Playing Large Pairs

Let's look a little closer at a pair of queens (and similar hands) on third street. If you hold

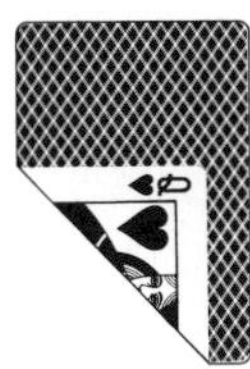

in early position, you should probably not raise if you are in a game where your raise will fail to cut down the field. In fact, if in a good, loose game, you choose to raise only with hands like

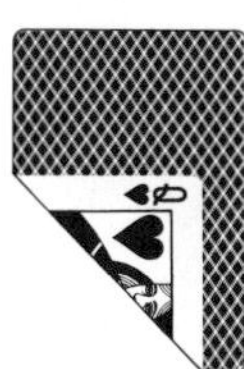

where your kicker is now a straight flush card or

that play well in large multiway pots, there would be nothing wrong with that.

To see why this is correct you must ask yourself when you are in a game like this, "What am I trying to accomplish by raising?"

For your raise with Q♥7♣Q♦ to be correct, you must be able to limit the pot to only a small number of players. If you can't do this, then you prefer to get in cheaply and make a decision on a later street as to how the hand should be played. It would be different if you could limit the field and thus frequently win without improving. But once the game is loose that's usually not the case.

Look at it this way. Suppose you raise with Q♥7♣Q♦, several players call, but your raise causes another player with

to fold. Are you happy that he folded?

If you were heads-up you might be happy that the T♠3♣3♦ folded. But once many players are in, you have to improve anyway, and the T♠3♣3♦ is only going to hurt you if he improves to at least three-of-a-kind while *you also improve to a lesser hand.* So if you knew your raise with the Q♥7♣Q♦would force the T♠3♣3♦ out, but a call will not, that's not a reason for you to raise.

(Of course it would be different if your kicker was a straight flush card. Now you should raise for some of the reasons that were discussed previously. A multiway pot no longer hurts you.)

An Adjustment Based on Player's Skill

There is another concept that we want to mention which is very important in good, loose games. Suppose a tough player to your right bets and there is a bad player to your left. If the situation is close between raising and calling, even with the scale normally tipping towards raising, you should not raise. This concept comes up on all betting rounds.

Having the bad player on your left should turn some raises into calls if you think that the raise will knock him out. In other words, on a close decision, be less likely to knock out a bad player behind you, especially if your raise is likely to leave you heads-up with a good player.

This idea is especially obvious on the last betting round. Let's say a good player bets and you have close to the nuts, but not the nuts. It's a mistake to raise him if your raise will shut a player out because the good player may now fold (or reraise). Why not get the call from the weak opponent on your left? You have a better chance than normal for the overcall, so go for it.

This concept is generally true on other rounds as well. There are some exceptions where you happen to have the kind of hand that really needs to get heads-up, but in general most players raise too often in these situations, thus not giving the weak player behind them a chance to call.

Again, if it is very important to get heads-up, then definitely try to do it. But if you have a hand that could be played either way, and you are leaning towards raising, if there is a bad player to your left (and even more so if the original bettor is a good player), just call and keep the bad player in.

There are two reasons for doing this. The obvious one is that when you get to play against a bad player, he's going to make mistakes against you.

There is also a second reason which very few players know to take into account. It has to do with what is known as a protected pot.[5] When you keep a bad player in on a close decision, you won't have to guess as much when a good player bets. He is far less likely to bluff because he knows that even if you fold, the other guy will call. This will have the effect of slowing him down, and you should take advantage of that.

You can sometimes reverse this concept when a bad player is in the hand. Suppose in an unraised multiway pot you have

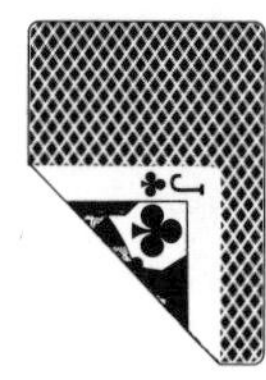

and you are the bring-in, and on fourth street you catch the

You check, a good player who has caught either a king or a queen bets, and a bad player calls. You should check-raise because it will be difficult for the good player to put you on a bluff since you are check raising not only him, but the bad player as well. And, you both know that the bad player will call you all the way.

---

[5] See *Sklansky on Poker* for more discussion.

By making this check-raise the good player won't try to get fancy with you. Not only will he throw away a pair smaller than your jacks (on fifth street), he might even muck a hand like

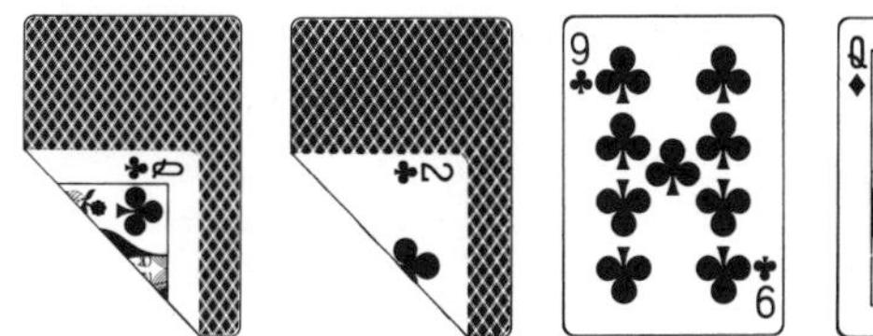

on fifth street and allow you to play the bad player heads-up. So by reversing this process you can sometimes take advantage of those times when the good player knows that you're not going to bluff the bad player.

Playing in Loose Games

Afterthought

It is true that if you play your normal tough game and assume that your opponents are playing well you should still win money in these easy loose games. But you won't win as much as you would if you made some adjustments.

The right strategy to beat loose games is very different than what many people think. The idea is not to immediately punish someone because you happen to have an edge. It is often correct to wait till a later round where your edge might be bigger to make your move. On the other hand, you may discover that your advantage has disappeared and you will be happy that you did not put in those extra bets earlier.

Bad players who play too many hands and go too far with their hands are ideal opponents. But you must make significant adjustments to exploit them to the fullest. This includes what hands you play, which hands you raise with and which hands you don't, and how you play those hands on the later streets.

It's always important to keep in mind that when the pots become very large the most important aspect to your strategy should be to win them. However, as we pointed out in the text, winning some of these hands is not just a matter of betting. Sometimes, as we have shown, it may be best not to bet at all so that you can try for a raise on the next round.

To conclude this section we want to point out that there is no shortage of loose games. In fact, at the time of this writing, the majority of stud games in cardrooms around the country are of the loose variety. Of course, on average, the small limit games are looser than the higher limit games (with the possible exception of some very high limit games that have a very large ante structure), and the quality of games does vary with location. But, if you understand the ideas in this section you should be able to exploit these games to the maximum whenever you find yourself sitting with weak players who play too many hands and go too far with them.

Part Five

Playing in Other Non-Standard Games

Playing in Other Non-Standard Games

Introduction

This text is designed for the medium limit games, most specifically the $15-$30 limit with a $2 ante and a $5 bring-in, up through the $30-$60 limit with a $5 ante and $10 bring-in. In addition, we are thinking of a game with a couple of very good players, but also several weaker ones. In general, the play is not too tight, nor is it extremely loose. In other words, we are talking about a typical seven-card stud game at medium limits that you would find in a major cardroom in either Nevada, California, New Jersey, or elsewhere.

Unfortunately, not all games are played as described above. Some forms of seven-card stud play somewhat differently mainly because of the way they are structured, or because they are either very loose or extremely tight. That is, the ante and betting limits may be different, or the players themselves may not play in what we would consider a typical fashion.

In any case, these games require some changes in strategy to win the optimal amount. (See the previous section on "Playing in Loose Games.") Of course, most of the concepts which we've already discussed and will discuss still apply. But there are some changes that need to be pointed out.

Playing in Spread Limit Games

Most small limit games in Nevada and elsewhere are spread limit games. A typical spread limit game is $1-$4, but $1-$3 and to a lesser extent $1-$5 are also popular.

In the $1-$4 game, there generally is no ante, but the low card has to bring it in for 50 cents. Any bets or raises on all betting rounds can be as little as $1, as much as $4, or any (practical) amount in between. For instance, after the low card brings it in for 50 cents, the next player has the option to either throw the hand away, call the 50 cents, raise as much as $4 (in some games $3.50 to make the total bet $4.00 even), or raise a lesser amount. The other two games mentioned are structured similarly.

The main reason we are discussing these games is simply for completeness. The fact is that anyone who reads and studies this book should be able to quickly advance from the low-limit games. But if you are on a very small bankroll, these games should be able to "pump you up" (in spite of the high rake) if played properly.

The basic change in a game like $1-$4 is that since the bring-in is just 50 cents and you probably are the best player at the table, you should come in for 50 cents with a fair number of hands. Even though you are not getting very good *pot* odds, your *implied* odds should be excellent, especially against bad players.

If you have a decent hand on third street you probably should raise, but not necessarily the full amount, especially if you are the first one in. *You want to raise an amount large enough so that the players behind you are not correct to call, but not so much that they will fold.* That is, instead of being a game of knocking people out, small limit stud becomes a game of trapping your opponent.

For instance, in the $1-$4 game, if you have

and the person on your right comes in for 50 cents, you should probably make it $2. People still will call with hands that they shouldn't, but if you make it the maximum immediately, many of the same people will correctly fold these hands. Give them a chance to make a mistake.

If a lot of players have already come in for 50 cents and you have two kings, you now should go ahead and raise the maximum amount. Remember, you are holding a hand that plays best against a small number of opponents. Raise to get a few of them out of the pot.

Other than this, there are not too many changes, except to realize that you are in a game against bad players who typically play too many hands and go too far with their hands. So on the later streets, if you have a hand that you are going to bet, always bet the maximum. Also, don't semi-bluff as often in these games since your opponents are much less likely to fold. Finally, if you don't think you have the best hand, especially in a heads-up pot, you usually should just check and frequently fold on an early street if you are charged the maximum and the pot is small. You are usually not getting the right odds to chase. Stay away from fancy plays, especially the ones that assume your opponents can think.

Playing in Tightly Structured Games

When we say "tightly structured games," we mean games where the structure makes tight play the right strategy and we are referring mainly to the \$5-\$10 and \$10-\$20 limits. For instance, the \$10-\$20 limit has a \$1 ante and a \$2 bring-in, and the first raise is to a total of \$10. (The first raise used to be to a total of \$7, but this form is only rarely spread anymore.) A \$5-\$10 game is similarly structured.

Compared to the \$15-\$30 limits, there is proportionately less starting money in the pot. When someone raises on third street in the \$10-\$20 game, he is raising to 10 times the size of the ante. This means that if it is a full raise to you, you need to be tighter than you would be in the \$15-\$30 game, assuming everything else is equal because in the \$15-\$30 game the raiser is raising only 7½ times the ante.

However, coming in for the bring-in in a tightly structured game is cheaper proportionately than in the \$15-\$30 game. So you can be a little looser coming in for this small amount. If you are in a game where there has not yet been any raise, it would be fairly common for you to call and then throw your hand away for a raise. This should happen only occasionally in a bigger game but should occur more often in these games.

If a lot of bad players are at your table, you should be limping in with even more hands (as in the \$1-\$4 game). But even for \$2, it is important to stay away from hands that won't do well in multiway pots. For example, usually don't limp in with

especially if one of your cards is out. You would prefer to have

or perhaps two suited high cards in the hole, particularly if one of the high cards is an ace (and your hand is live).

You should also frequently limp if first in with a big pair if the game is playing fairly tight in an attempt to trap people. If someone then raises you should usually reraise unless their upcard is higher than your pair. (Now you should frequently fold.)

There is little difference on the later streets, except that some of your opponents will have a tendency to play a bit tighter. If there is no raise on third street, in which case the pot figures to be smaller, you should take that into account. In other words, you also should play tighter.

By the way, tightly structured games are excellent games for winning money, especially if several poor players are present. In addition, if you are playing well, your fluctuations when compared to other forms of seven-card stud should be surprisingly small.

Playing in High Limit Games

There are several differences in play as you move to higher limits. Not only are the antes proportionately larger (sometimes much larger), but also many of your opponents will play quite well. In addition, the play tends to be faster and more aggressive.

For instance, the $15-$30 has a $2.00 ante. The $30-$60 game with a $5 ante would be like the $15-$30 game with a $2.50 ante. The $50-$100 game with a $10 ante would be like a $15-$30 game with a $3 ante. And the $100-$200 game with a $25 ante would be like a $15-$30 game with a $3.75 ante.

Taking the extreme case of the $100-$200 game that has a $25 ante and a $25 bring-in, it would be correct to come in for $25 with many hands if you knew the bet would not be raised. Because it is correct to call the $25 bring-in with numerous hands, it becomes important not to let other people do it. Therefore, you have to raise with many hands that you may think are only worth calling, especially if no one else is in yet.

If someone else raises and he is (correctly) raising with many hands, if you have a decent hand that you are going to play, you usually should reraise. Here's an example. The player on your right raises with an ace up and you have:

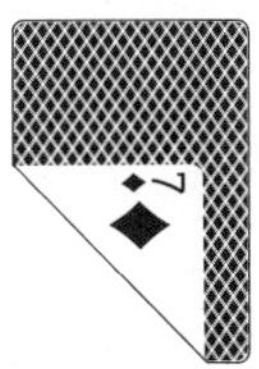

This is almost an automatic reraise. Even if you knew your opponent had two aces, reraising with your pair of queens would be only a slightly bad play. This is because by reraising, you at least get a chance to play heads-up and be only a little more than a 2-to-1 dog. If your opponent does not have aces, failing to reraise is an absolutely terrible play. Therefore, reraising is either slightly wrong or tremendously right.

So with this big ante, when other people know how to play and thus raise a lot, you must do the same. That is, raise and reraise often if these bets knock people out. On the other hand, if your raise or reraise probably won't have the desired effect, then you might be better off calling and look to get your raise in on a later street. For example, if an ace raises, a six calls, a nine calls, and a four calls, and you have two queens, it is doubtful that you can eliminate anyone. In this situation, it is better just to call. Now you may have an opportunity to knock someone out on fifth street.

To continue with this example, suppose the player with the ace up has started with a three-flush, and on fourth street he makes a small pair. If on fifth street he is still high on board and checks after catching a blank, and someone between you and him bets, your raise should get him to fold, and you will usually want him to do so even though you have the better hand.

Also, since the pots get so big, semi-bluffing should be done less, as you have virtually no chance of winning the pot. Betting your threatening board in the hope that you might catch another good card, which will make your opponent fold, also should be done less if you don't think you have the best hand.

In addition, as the pots get big and someone bets, not only on third street but on the later streets as well, you constantly have to raise to knock people out, even though you might not think you have the best hand. This is because you are likely to be in a situation where a raise changes your chances of winning from, let's say, 25 percent to 35 percent. Because of the large pots, this small increase in winning makes raising worthwhile even though it will cost you extra money more often than not.

Another thing to keep in mind is that high-limit seven-card stud is a highly fluctuating game. This means that even if you play well at these limits, to ensure survival, you need a big bankroll. (Many high limit stud players refer to their game as a "roller coaster ride." They have good reason to make this statement.)

One skill that is especially needed in a high-limit game is the ability to put your mind into the heads of your opponents and know what they are thinking. (See the section on "Psychology" later in this book and in *The Theory of Poker* by David Sklansky.)

Basically, high-limit poker is a game of trying to knock people out. This often means raising with hands that may not seem like they are worth a raise; these raises are necessary, as you might make something that winds up winning the pot because you have eliminated opponents. The extra bets that you can win or save (by not raising players out) are almost never as important as increasing your chances of having the best hand when all the cards are out. And if worrying about saving one or two bets keeps you from raising, then you ought not to be playing in these games at all.

Playing in Extremely Tight Games

Extremely tight games actually can be quite profitable. In fact, they conceivably could be as profitable (per hour) as loose games. If they become very tight, the ante (even at the $15-$30 limit) is big enough that if you can start stealing it a lot, you can achieve an excellent win rate.

You should do a lot of raising when no one else is in yet, especially if you have one of the two highest cards showing. In fact, in some of these games, it is always correct to raise when your upcard meets this criteria.

However, if someone else raises, throw away hands that you normally might have played. For example, if an ace raises and you have

throw your hand away most of the time.

If you raise and get called, be less likely to push the hand any further. For instance, suppose you raise with

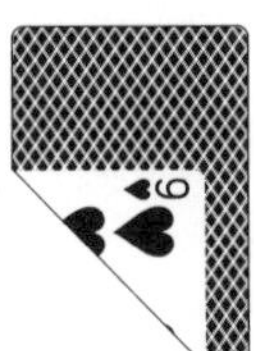

and the T♦ calls. Now you catch the A♦ and your opponent catches the (offsuit) 9♠, you probably should check and fold if he bets. This is a better strategy (in these extremely tight games) than betting one more time, as you normally would in more typical games. Usually, you are being called with such a good hand that your opponent most likely is planning to stay all the way to the river. In other words, be less likely to "push it" just because you caught a scare card. However, if you catch a *very* scary card, you can bet, especially since your opponents are playing extremely tight. But if you catch anything other than that, you should check and fold if there is a bet, unless you have a legitimate hand.

These extremely tight games do occur. The most common place is in tournaments, and the techniques just discussed are thus very effective in tournaments. (See the tournament sections in *Sklansky on Poker* by David Sklansky and *Gambling Theory and Other Topics* by Mason Malmuth as well as *Poker Tournament Strategies* by Sylvester Suzuki.)

Playing in Short-Handed Games

Unlike hold 'em, short-handed stud doesn't require that much change in your strategy. At least theoretically it doesn't. The reason is because, although on average it takes less of a hand to win, there is less money in the pot in antes, so if you try to steal the antes too often your risk versus reward ratio changes. Compare this to hold 'em where the amount of money in the pot stays constant due to the blind structure that hold 'em employs.

The bottom line is that those who try to steal too many antes in short-handed stud games are risking too much to win too little. So if you stuck to your normal, fairly tight game you really wouldn't be hurting yourself. It might feel like you are giving up too many antes without a fight, but all it takes is one hand to get most of them back. And when you do in fact have that good hand you're going to be up against that aggressive player who is getting involved when he shouldn't. (Compare this to hold 'em where [if you are in the blind] you must make sure that you call enough to stop someone who raises every time from making a profit.)

The reason, however, why short-handed poker can be difficult for people who are trying to learn poker from books or who are used to full games, is simply that many ring game players never learn how to play poor to mediocre hands well. This is because the need to do that doesn't come up very often in full games. For instance, the ability to play your low card well against somebody who makes an automatic raise in the steal position is not very important if you're used to playing in loose eight-handed seven-card stud games. This is because in this type of game you will very rarely be in that situation. Thus, if you are in general a good stud player but play that particular situation poorly, you receive only a very small penalty, and you might very well be a big winner even with that weakness.

That is the reason why some people do poorly when playing seven-card stud short-handed, but do well in ring games. What they don't realize is that they also have negative results in the ring games in those few situations that are analogous to short-handed. They just don't come up that much. Thus, if you do learn to play well short-handed, it will also help you in those similar situations which occur in ring games. And it might allow you to take advantage of a profitable short game situation every now and then.

Lets get specific. In ring games, you can almost always make the assumption that your opponents have, on average, rather good hands. This means that you can avoid the lower end of the mediocre hands. But in a short-handed game where other people are playing quite a few more pots, you will frequently encounter situations where your hand, as bad as it is, is wrong to fold. Again, this is a situation that if you handled poorly in ring games, wouldn't cost you very much. But since it comes up so often in short-handed games you can't just ignore it.

Against loose, aggressive players you must not just meekly call with your poor hands. You must occasionally splash around, raising with hands that seem like they are barely worth calling, in order to prevent your opponents from having a big edge from their semi-bluffs. For instance, you might have only a small pair, and your opponent, showing a deuce as his door card keeps on betting. Specifically on fifth street you have

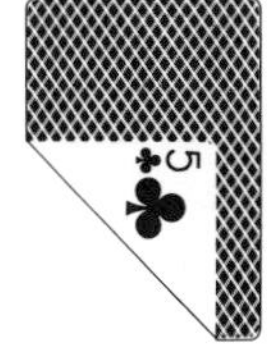

and your opponent could has

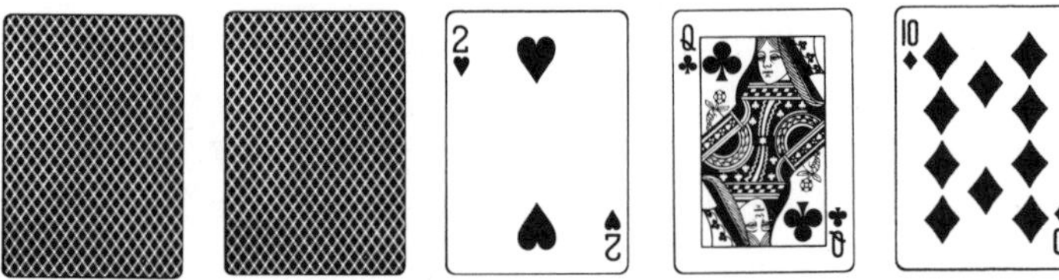

The right play may be to raise on fifth street.

A play like this has one big advantage. The bettor may not have any pair at all, and will certainly fold. If you just call him, he might pair up while you don't improve and thus lose the pot. In a full game you wouldn't make this play because it would be highly likely that you are beaten. But in a short-handed game where it is not nearly as likely, it should be a major part of your arsenal.

Furthermore, you should be making some of these loose, aggressive bets on the later streets even against players who don't play as we have just described. That is, if you are against someone who will raise only with a reasonable raising hand and who requires a legitimate calling hand to keep playing, you should fire away. This is especially true if his board looks ragged.

Earlier in the text we gave guidelines on how to play against a late position raiser when the raiser is first in, and you act after him. (See "Part Three: Miscellaneous Concepts" — "Defending Against the Possible Ante Steal" on page 101.) This should be your starting guideline against most players except, as we have already pointed out, since the initial pot is smaller, you won't need to defend quite as much.

However, if you find yourself against players who are playing fancy, that is loose and aggressive, you've got to throw in raises with hands that are well below those that you would normally raise with. In some cases, below those that you would even call with. There is simply no way to go into all of the details, and all of the types of situations that could come up. But if you just keep this one thing in mind and use your judgement, experience and your knowledge of poker concepts, you will be well on your way to playing properly.

Playing in Other Non-Standard Games

Afterthought

As you can see, the ideas and concepts presented in this section are built upon those that have been covered earlier in the book. For instance, when playing in a spread limit game you can play some weak drawing hands up front due to the large implied odds that you expect, as long as there is not much raising.

On the other hand, there are a large number of variations of non-standard games that this form of poker has to offer. We have just touched on a small number of them. However, the general ideas presented in this text should allow you to successfully attack almost any form of seven-card stud. Once again, we strongly urge you to read *The Theory of Poker* by David Sklansky to gain a fuller understanding of the general concepts underlying seven-card stud and other games.

Part Six
Other Skills

Other Skills

Introduction

There are two additional areas that play a major role in winning at seven-card stud (as well as at all forms of poker). They are reading hands and psychology.

Reading hands is both an art and a science. The same is true for correct applications of psychology at the poker table. In both instances, you must know your opponents. More specifically, the better you understand how your opponents think and thus how they play, the better you will be able to choose the correct strategies to use against them.

Even when you are not in a pot, it is still important to pay attention to what is going on. By doing so, you will begin to understand how your different opponents play their hands in different situations and what tactics they are most likely to try. Also, you can get a feel for how they think. You will see what they handle easily and what confuses them, and you will get an idea of what strategies work best against them.

Keep in mind that the concepts discussed in this section cannot be mastered quickly. Like many other skills at the stud table, reading hands and applying psychology take a while to learn and require a great deal of experience. But once mastered, they will become significant factors in your winning play. And for those of you who make it to the very big games (against the world champions), you must become expert in these two areas to have any chance of success.

Reading Hands

There are three techniques for reading hands in seven-card stud. Most commonly, you analyze the meaning of an opponent's check, bet, or raise, and you look at the exposed cards and try to judge from them what his entire hand might be. You then combine the plays he has made *throughout the hand* with the exposed cards and come to a determination about his most likely hand.

In other words, you use logic to read hands. You interpret your opponents' plays on each round and note the cards that appear on the board, paying close attention to the order in which they appear. You then put these two pieces of evidence together — the plays and the cards on the board — to draw a conclusion about an opponent's most likely hand.

Sometimes you can put an opponent on a specific hand quite early. However, in general, it's a mistake to do this and then stick to your initial conclusion no matter how things develop. A player who raises on third street with a small upcard and then raises again after catching only small cards may have a big pair in the hole, but he also may be on a draw and is trying for a free card. Drawing a narrow, irreversible conclusion early, can lead to costly mistakes later (because you either give that free card or bet when your opponent makes his hand).

What you should do is put an opponent on a variety of hands at the start of play, and as play progresses, eliminate some of those hands based on his later play and on the cards he catches. Through this process of elimination, you should have a good idea of what that opponent has (or is drawing to) when the last card is dealt.

Suppose, for instance, that on third street an opponent calls after you raise. On fourth street he catches a small suited card and raises after you bet, but when you check to him on fifth street, he also checks after catching a blank. It is now very likely that he is on a flush draw and was buying a free card. If he catches a flush card on sixth street, you should not bet into him. If he catches a blank on sixth street, you should bet and then probably check on the river, unless you think he also has made a pair and will call with it. However, if you were also on a flush draw and have missed it, you may now want to bet, since a reasonable chance exists that you can pick up the pot.

At the end of the hand, it becomes especially crucial to have a good idea of what your opponent has. The more accurately you can read hands on the end, the better you can determine your chances of having your opponent beat. This, of course, helps you in deciding how to play your own hand.

In practice, most players at least try to determine whether an opponent has a bad hand, a mediocre hand, a good hand, or a great hand. Let's say your opponent bets on the end. Usually when a person bets, it represents either a bluff, a good hand, or a great hand, but not a mediocre hand. If your opponent had a mediocre hand, he probably would check. If you have only a mediocre hand, you must determine what the chances are that your opponent is bluffing and whether those chances warrant a call in relation to the pot odds. For example, most players will not bet two small pair on the end. This is the mediocre type hand that they hope will win the pot in a showdown.

We have seen that one way to read hands is to start by considering a variety of possible hands an opponent might have and then to eliminate some of those possibilities as the hand develops. A complimentary way to read hands is to work backward. For instance, someone with a small card up cold calls a raise and a reraise by a king and an ace. He catches nothing special on fourth, fifth, and sixth streets, but raises on sixth street. Now you think back on his play in earlier rounds. Since it does not seem possible that he would have called this far with something like a three-flush or a small pair, you have to suspect that he is rolled up.

Here is another example. Suppose on sixth street, a player who called a raise on third street has

Someone with a king in the door and a small pair on board bets, another player who has caught an ace on sixth street raises, and now this person calls the raise. What is his hand?

First, notice that it is not likely that this person just has queens or even queens up (even though it is likely that he started with two queens). Given the small pair showing to go along with the probable pair of kings, plus the raise from the other player who has just caught an ace, he would have little chance of winning with queens up, as he is likely to be against two players who each have a higher two pair. Also, if he has three-of-a-kind, he probably would reraise since he is likely to be against aces up at best. This means that even though the player in question probably started with a pair of queens and may now in fact have queens up, he also figures to have a flush draw. Expect to find the Q♣, plus some other club, in the hole.

Here's a third example. On third street, suppose several people limp in and the pot is then raised by a strong player with the 6♦ up. On fourth street, the strong player catches another diamond, but one of the original limpers in an early position catches an ace, bets, and gets several callers between him and the third-street raiser. If the third-street raiser now raises again, there is a good chance that he had three to a straight flush or at least a high three-flush to start with and now has a four-flush with three cards to come. This would be especially true if the fourth-street bettor is not the type of player who would reraise to eliminate those between him and the strong player. On the other hand, if the initial fourth-street bettor had caught a high card below an ace, it would be conceivable for the strong player to be raising with a bigger pair in the hole.

Let us now look at another technique. When you can't actually put a person on a hand, but have reduced his possible holdings to a limited number, you try to use mathematics to determine the chances of his having certain hands rather than others. Then you decide what kind of hand you must have to continue playing.

Sometimes you can use a mathematical procedure based on Bayes' Theorem to determine the chances that an opponent has one or another hand. After deciding on the kinds of hands your opponent would be betting in a particular situation, you determine the probability of your opponent holding each of those hands. Then you compare those probabilities.

Here's an example. Suppose an opponent, who is a tight player, starts with a medium card up and catches a third suited upcard on sixth street that is also an ace. Now he bets. You hold a hidden three-of-a-kind and are trying to determine whether you should raise or just call. If many of that suit already were exposed, especially on third street — meaning that it would be unlikely for your opponent to have a flush — you should raise when he bets, since it is much more probable that you are against aces up rather than a flush. Conversely, if the flush possibilities are live and you think this is a possible hand for your opponent to have been trying to make, you should just call and raise only if you make a full house or better on the river.

Knowing that it is slightly more likely that your opponent has one kind of holding versus another does not in itself tell you how you should proceed in the play of the hand. (You may still be right in playing the hand as if he has the less likely holding. This concept is discussed in greater detail in *Getting the Best of It* by David Sklansky.) Nevertheless, the more you know about the chances of an opponent having one hand rather than another when he bets or raises, the easier it is for you to decide whether to fold, call, or raise.

Here's another example. Suppose on third street you have

You raise, and an opponent behind you reraises with an eight up. On fourth street, both you and your opponent pair your door cards, and he bets. If you think your opponent is about equally likely to have a big pair in the hole (which is very unlikely to be aces) as another eight, you should at least call. If you now catch an eight on fifth street and your opponent bets again, your play is to raise if you know this opponent would still bet if he had only two pair. This is because it is now much more (mathematically) likely that you have the best hand, since you see another eight.

Finally, as this last example shows, you need to complement mathematical conclusions with what you know about a player. For example, some players almost always will just call with a hidden big pair in the hole, especially if it is live, and try to raise you on a later street. In this case, if the player calls and then raises on fourth or fifth street after catching blanks, he is much more likely to have a big pair in the hole than he is to be rolled up. This is particularly true if the raise comes on fourth street.

Another important factor in reading hands and deciding how to play your own hand is the number of players in the pot. Players tend to play their hands much more straightforwardly in multiway pots. This is also true if there are several players yet to act. So if a player bets (especially with a non-threatening board) in either of these situations, you can be quite sure he's got a real hand. (We only devote one paragraph to this concept because it is so simply stated, not because it isn't critical.)

Psychology

What we mean by the psychology of poker is getting into your opponents' heads, analyzing how they think, figuring out what they think you think, and even determining what they think you think they think. In this sense, the psychology of poker is an extension of reading opponents' hands, and it is also an extension of using deception in the way you play your own hand.

Here is an example. On third street, you have the highest upcard, and are in a late position, have little, and raise trying to steal the antes. You get reraised by a strong player who has the low card up and who knows that you automatically would try to steal in this position. Since you know that he knows you automatically would try to steal, his reraise does not necessarily mean that he has a very good hand. Consequently, since your opponent also may be semi-bluffing, the correct play could be for you to raise back and then to bet again on fourth and fifth streets if necessary.

This brings up another point. The above play works because you are against a strong player whose thinking makes sense. A weak player is a different story. Just as you can't put a weak player on a hand, you can't put him on a thought either.

Very sophisticated seven-card stud can go even beyond this third level. For example, an early-position player (who is also high) catches a suited card on fourth street, he bets, and a strong player calls him. On fifth street, this player catches a blank and bets again. His opponent, who thinks this player is probably on a flush draw (perhaps because he just called with the high upcard on third street), may now raise with a medium pair on fifth street. His opponent may realize this and raise back, trying to represent a strong hand. The initial raiser may now comprehend this possibility and call his opponent down. When the hand is over, assuming that the flush card does not come, his calls will look fantastic to some opponents, if he actually is against a flush draw.

Conversely, if it turns out that the first bettor really has a hand, the calls will look like a "sucker play."

At the expert level of seven-card stud, the "skill" of trying to outwit your opponent sometimes can extend to so many levels that your judgement may begin to fail. However, in ordinary play against good players, you should think at least up to the third level. First, think about what your opponent has. Second, think about what your opponent thinks you have. And third, think about what your opponent thinks you think he has. Only when you are playing against weak players, who might not bother to think about what you have and who almost certainly don't think about what you think they have, does it not necessarily pay to go through such thought processes. Against all others, it is crucial to successful play.

Several other important ideas play major roles in the psychology of poker. To begin with, when an opponent bets on the end in a situation where he is sure you are going to call, he is not bluffing. For example, suppose that you bet when all the cards are out and a player raises you. It is rare to find an opponent who is capable of raising on the end as a bluff. This is particularly true in seven-card stud if your opponent is aware that you know you should just about always call when the pots get so big. Similarly, if you raise when all the cards are out and your opponent reraises, you usually should fold, unless your hand can beat some of the legitimate hands with which he might be raising. (But beware of the player who knows you are capable of these folds.)

However, this is not true of fifth or sixth street. Tough players will raise on these streets if they hold a mediocre hand that has some potential to become a very strong hand. An example is a medium pair that has now picked up a flush draw. Those of you who automatically fold when raised in these situations are giving up too much. This is especially true at the larger limits, where the games are usually tougher.

A corollary to the principle we are discussing is that if your opponent bets when there appears to be a *good* chance that you will fold, he may *very well* be bluffing. What this means in practice is that if your opponent bets in a situation where he thinks he might be able to get away with a bluff, you have to give more consideration to calling him, even with a mediocre hand.

An example is when no one bets on the fourth card and no one catches a scare card on fifth street. If one of your opponents now bets, and he is the type of player who would try to pick up the pot with nothing, it may be correct to call (or raise) with a relatively weak hand.

In deciding whether to bet, it is equally important to consider what your opponent thinks *you* have. If your opponent suspects a strong hand, you should bluff more. However, you should not bet a fair hand for value in this situation.

An example would be when you raise on fourth street with two suited cards and now catch a blank on fifth street. If you check (on fifth street) but bet again on sixth street when you catch a third suited card, it is very hard for many of your opponents to call with only a pair. So bet your small pairs in this spot.

Conversely, if you know your opponent suspects that you are weak, you should not try to bluff, as you will get caught. But you should bet your fair hands for value. For example, if both you and your opponent checked on sixth street, you frequently can bet one big pair on the end for value. (Or in the previous example if you did *not* catch a suited card on sixth street after checking on fifth street you can again bet mediocre hands for value from that point on.)

Varying your play and making an "incorrect" play intentionally are also part of the psychology of seven-card stud, because you are trying to affect the thinking of your opponents for future hands. For example, you occasionally can reraise on third street a late-position player with a high card up, who may be on a steal, when you hold something like a small three-flush (especially if your hand is live). Assuming that your opponents see your hand in a showdown, they should be less inclined to steal against you in a similar situation. Also, you are taking advantage of the impression you created to get paid off later in the game when you have a legitimate reraising hand.

Another example of this type of play is to throw in an extra raise early with cards that don't really warrant it, in order to give the *illusion of action*. For instance, on third street, you can occasionally reraise a high card smaller than an ace with a hand like

especially if you are going to play this holding anyway. This play costs only a fraction of a bet in mathematical expectation, but gains you a tremendous amount in future action on subsequent hands. However, this play should probably not be made in loose games where you are against people who play too many hands and go too far with their hands, because you get excess action anyway.

There are also other ways you can affect your opponents' play on future hands in seven-card stud. For example, you may want to make what you think is a bad call if you believe this play will keep other players from "running over you." If you find that you have been forced to throw away your hand on the end two or three times in a row, you must be prepared to call the next time with a hand that you normally wouldn't call with. This is because you can assume that your opponents have noticed your folding and are apt to try to bluff you.

A less obvious situation where you should think of the future is to sometimes limp in early position on third street with a strong hand (such as a pair of kings with a king up) and then check it again on fourth (and perhaps fifth) street, even if there was no raise on third street. Not only may you catch someone stealing, but this check also might allow you to steal the pot in a future hand (when you limp in with a high card or a draw) when there has been no betting up to that point (especially when you catch an irrelevant card).

In general, you should evaluate any play you make on its merits alone, that is, on its expectation in a given situation. However, you occasionally might want to do something that is theoretically incorrect to create an impression for the future. Once you have opponents thinking one way, you can take advantage of that thinking later.

Finally, keep in mind that these types of plays will work against players who are good enough to try to take advantage of their new-found knowledge, but who are not good enough to realize that you know this, and that they should therefore ignore it. In seven-card stud, as in all poker games, there seems to be a large group of players who like to "realize things." You must know how these people think and whether they are thinking only on the level that you are giving them credit for. If they think on a still higher level, you have to step up to that next level. (Against really top players who often switch levels you must resort to Game Theory. See *The Theory of Poker* by David Sklansky.)

Other Skills

Afterthought

As we have just seen, reading hands and psychology are extremely important aspects of seven-card stud. Put another way, this game is too complex to play by rote. If you always play a certain hand in a certain position a certain way, your game can use a lot of improvement. You must take into account your opponents, how the current hand has been played, how former hands were played, your opponents' perceptions of you, and so on. If you don't consider these factors, you may be able to win, but you never will achieve expert status.

Many of the ideas in this section are most powerful against decent players — that is, players who play in predictable patterns and who are capable of realizing things when at the poker table, especially if they play "weak tight." Against bad players, straightforward play is usually the best approach, and against extremely good players, these ideas will only keep you about even with them.

Finally, some players put too much emphasis on the two topics just covered. They are certainly very important, but they are just some of the weapons that the expert has in his seven-card stud arsenal. Skill in reading hands and psychology, combined with all the other ideas and concepts that we have addressed, will produce a top player. But as we have stated before, this requires a great deal of thinking about the game and lots of experience playing seven-card stud.

Part Seven

Questions and Answers

Questions and Answers

Introduction

We have covered a great deal of material in this book. However, for many people, reading and learning can be two different things. Consequently, to help you retain some of the more significant ideas, we have reiterated them in a question-and-answer format.

We suggest that after you have read and studied the text, you try to answer the following questions. You probably will want to go over them many times. In addition, we suggest that you cover the answer that immediately follows the question. Only look at the solution after you have answered the question to the best of your ability.

Also, we want to point out that what follows is not a substitute for the text. In fact, some of the ideas in the text are not contained here. But enough material is included so that after you have thoroughly digested the text, the questions should help keep your seven-card stud game sharp.

Finally, the questions and answers are organized by topics covered in the text, so you can easily return to the appropriate section for a fuller explanation.

The Cards That Are Out

1. How much impact do the other cards that are out have?
   More than most people realize, especially in an eight-handed game.

2. Can you elaborate?
   In extreme cases you should throw the "best" hand away.

3. Example?
   You start with J♣J♠6♥, and both jacks and a six are out. A deuce brings it in, a five raises, and then three other people call. You should throw the hand away.

4. When would it be correct to play this hand with those cards out?
   If it had a good chance to steal the antes.

5. When else might you play?
   If you can get in cheaply in an unraised pot and one of the jacks is showing instead of the six.

6. What are you trying to do?
   Catch a scare card.

7. Are weak hands that are completely live, whether they are straight draws, pairs, or whatever, worth playing?
   Usually. However, a small pair with a small, unrelated kicker still should usually be thrown away if the bring-in was raised to a full bet.

8. What about a decent hand that is partially dead?
   It may not be worth playing.

9. What if it is almost completely dead?
   It is almost certainly not worth playing, even if it is probably the best starting hand.

10. What is normally an exception?
    Two aces or two kings, except against an ace showing.

11. What does this mean?
    You should be very aware of the cards that are out, especially on third street.

The Number of Players in the Pot

1. What should you do if you have a hand that prefers a small number of players rather than a lot of players?

   If you get a chance to knock people out, you should of course do it.

2. What if this is not possible?

   Proper strategy now may be to play your hand much differently than if you were able to limit the field.

3. What should you do if you have a hand that when played heads-up will increase your chances of winning from 20 to 40 percent?

   You should make an effort to achieve this status.

4. What if getting heads-up increased your chances of winning from 60 to 80 percent?

   The same is still true. That is, try to get heads-up.

5. What if you have a good hand that has much higher expectation heads-up and you can't get heads-up?

   Usually call instead of raise.

6. What if you have a weak hand that you would rather play heads-up and you can't achieve this?

   You should fold.

7. Example?

   You would want to play 7♣Q♠7♦ heads-up against a probable pair of jacks.

8. What if you have a live ace with a three-flush and the pot has been raised?

   Frequently reraise if your raise can get it heads-up.

9. What if you have two overcards over the raiser?

   You should always reraise.

10. What else might this reraise do for you?

    Help you get a free card.

Ante Stealing

1. What do we mean by "ante stealing?"

   Trying to win the antes by raising with a hand that figures to be in trouble if it is called.

2. What are your odds on an ante steal?

   In most games you are getting about 4-to-3.

3. How often does your steal have to work to show an immediate profit?

   About 40 percent of the time.

4. Do your chances need to be that good?

   No, you may win later on.

5. Is it usually worth a try to steal the antes if your chances of success are less than 40 percent?

   Yes.

6. When would this be particularly true?

   If the next card can win you the pot immediately.

7. Example?

   You raise with an ace and catch an ace.

8. How often will this happen?

   About 6 percent of the time.

9. Are there other ways of being able to gain equity on the next round?

   Yes.

10. How?

If the next card gives you a hand strong enough that it would be wrong for someone to call your bet on fourth street if he knew what your hole cards were.

11. Example?

You raise with A♠K♥9♦, and a pair smaller than kings calls you. If you catch an ace or a king, and your opponent knew that you had one of these cards in the hole he should fold, providing that he does not improve.

12. How much does this improve your chances?

About 12 percent.

13. What else?

You have another 6 percent chance of making open nines.

14. What does this mean?

You have almost an 18 percent chance of winning the pot on fourth street if your opponent will fold small pairs if you catch an ace or a king, or if you pair your door card, and you do even better if he doesn't fold against the ace or king.

15. When you catch a scare card, what type of hands are your opponents likely to throw away?

Hands made up of lower pairs than your board cards.

16. Example?

On fourth street your board is A♠Q♠. Your opponent is likely to throw away any hand up to two jacks.

17. What does this mean?

When you are on a steal, also consider how high your opponents' upcards are.

18. What's the bottom line?

    Raise with hands that have about a 30 percent chance of stealing if the game is at least moderately tight.

19. What does this usually mean?

    Hands having the highest card showing, with half decent cards in the hole; or the second highest upcard, with fair cards in the hole.

20. What if the game gets looser?

    Your hand needs to be progressively better to try to steal, even with the high card.

21. What if you are inexperienced?

    You should steal even less.

22. Why is an ace up especially good?

    With the exception of being rolled up, opponents never can have the hand that you are representing beat.

23. What if you don't have the highest upcard?

    You risk being reraised by the person who does.

24. What if this person is a good player?

    You may be reraised even if he does not have what he is representing.

25. What does this mean?

    Be less apt to steal the antes without the highest card showing, especially if there is one or more aggressive or tough players showing higher cards yet to act.

26. Why is the second highest upcard frequently a better raising hand than it appears?

    Because it will appear that your hand is real.

27. Should you be willing to reraise when you hold the highest upcard, but don't necessarily have the raiser beat?

Yes.

28. With what hands would you make this play?

With a three-flush or any of the other playable hands that you should at least call with. Now you should sometimes reraise.

29. Why is this play correct?

You are holding a legitimate hand that has a good chance of beating your opponent.

30. Is it correct to steal up front?

"Occasionally," but only if the game is tight, and generally only when you have the highest card showing.

31. Can you be more specific?

You should usually limit your steal raises (in an early position) to those times when you have an ace or a king up.

32. What if the game is loose?

Trying to steal up front is usually a mistake.

33. What if the highest card is held by a player who folds a lot?

If he also doesn't reraise without a bigger pair than he possibly faces, you can raise as a steal with the second highest card from an early position.

34. Do you make these raises at random?

No. They should be based on the strength of your hand and on the other upcards.

35. What if you are facing duplicate cards?

You can raise more.

36. Example?

    Your hand is <u>T♦Q♥</u>K♠. The game is moderately tight, you are in an early position, and there are two aces behind you, but they are not held by strong players.

37. What if someone else has already limped in?

    You should usually not try to steal.

38. When is one time not to steal with the highest card showing, even when you are not in an early position?

    When the game is loose and you have terrible hole cards.

39. Another time when you should not steal?

    When your upcard is duplicated elsewhere.

40. What are the problems with a duplicated upcard?

    A. You must now worry about the opponent with the same upcard.

    B. Your opponent knows that it is now harder for you to have the hand that you are representing.

    C. Even if you do have this hand, it is harder to improve.

41. Can you steal too much?

    Yes.

42. Elaborate.

    Suppose you are in a game where at first you can steal the antes virtually every time. If you overdo it, your opponents will begin to realize what is happening.

43. What are the problems with this?

    First, you will be called a lot. Second, your opponents will start to reraise you.

44. What else should you always remember when ante stealing?

    Many players want to believe you are stealing.

45. Why is this important?
    It gives them an excuse to play.

46. So what's the conclusion?
    Steal slightly less frequently than what might appear to be correct. That is, throw away your worst hands (when you have the high card up) to keep your opponents trained to fold more often than they should.

47. Give some examples of minimum ante-stealing hands.
    A. Three cards higher than the next highest upcard, such as A♣7♠9♥ if no one else has a card as high as a seven.
    B. Any kind of gut-shot draw.
    C. Any kind of two-card flush draw such as 6♥5♥A♠ if all your cards are live.

48. What do you need to keep in mind?
    To play this loose, your opponents must be folding a lot.

49. If you are on a steal or semi-steal, and someone raises, should you throw your hand away?
    It depends on what your cards are, what your opponent's upcard is, and how the reraiser plays.

50. Examples?
    A. You raise with Q♣9♠J♥ and a seven reraises. You would definitely call.
    B. If you have 2♣2♠Q♦ you would call the seven.
    C. If you raised with 9♠7♦A♠ and a jack reraises, you should fold.

51. If you have 2♣2♠Q♦ and a king reraises, what should you do?
    Probably fold.

52. What are the exceptions?

If your opponent is prone to bluff, or if your hand is extremely live.

53. More examples?

A. If you raise with 9♣8♠A♥ and a five reraises you should call because you may have three overcards.

B. If you raised with a ten up (and something like seven-six in the hole) and a queen reraises, you should fold since you have no overcards.

54. Should you ever not call the reraise from the five with the 9♣8♠A♥?

You should fold if you think you are against a big pair in the hole.

55. After the low card brings it in, if everyone folds and you are last, how often should you raise?

Approximately 85 percent of the time against a typical player, but somewhat less against an expert.

56. What do you do the other 15 percent of the time?

Usually call.

57. When should you fold?

Fold only if:

A. You have absolutely nothing, and your opponent is extremely loose and aggressive.

B. You have nothing, it is obvious, and your opponent is a very good player.

58. Give an example of the second condition?

A six brings it in. You have a seven up. Two sevens are out. It comes around to you, and you have absolutely nothing. Fold against a good player.

59. When do you just call a bad player (when he is low and you are last)?

When you have next to nothing and this player will almost always call if you raise.

60. Why is this call correct?

Because you are getting more than 4-to-1.

61. When is this especially true?

Against a very aggressive player who will either reraise or fold.

62. Example?

You are last and have 3♣2♦K♠. No other king is showing, a five brings it in, and everyone else folds. You should call a loose player, but raise a tough player.

63. What if a couple of kings are out?

You usually would just call against the tough player (although folding isn't that bad a play).

64. Why do you usually call even when your hand is terrible?

You may get the opportunity to catch one or two scare cards which could allow you to win the pot with a bet.

65. With your worst hands, what must you be prepared to do if your opponent bets (on a later street)?

Give up quickly.

66. If you have raised on third street, get called, and you don't have much on fourth street, what should you do?

Either bet or check and fold.

67. What is almost never right in this spot?

To check and call.

68. What is an exception?

    You have a pretty good hand, but your opponent has caught the type of card that makes it correct to check and call.

Three-of-a-Kind "Wired"

1. How do you play rolled up trips?
   It usually doesn't matter very much how you play these hands if you are the first one in.

2. If you have rolled up trips and several people have called, what should you do?
   Raise.

3. What should you do if you are the first one in and hold three-of-a-kind?
   Whether small or large, either calling or raising may be okay.

4. What should be the deciding factor?
   The type of game, either loose or tight, aggressive or passive.

5. Should you ever raise with three-of-a-kind if you are up front?
   Yes.

6. What is a reason to raise with this hand in early position?
   Getting more money in the pot can "tie on" other players.

7. When should you be more inclined to raise with rolled up trips?
   If your trips are small.

8. How should you usually play small trips?
   Fast. Be sure to reraise if already raised, and frequently raise if there are many big cards behind you. Both of these raises will encourage a big pot.

9. What is one reason to reraise a probably big pair with a rolled up hand?
   To make him think you have a bigger pair in the hole.

10. What happens if the player holding the big pair makes a hidden two pair?

    You will often get three bets out of him on either fifth or sixth street.

11. What if he pairs his board (not his door card)?

    You usually will get two bets that round.

12. What should you consider when deciding to raise or reraise with three-of-a-kind?

    Whether the raise may give your hand away.

13. Example?

    A queen raised and then an ace reraised. If you come over the top, you essentially are announcing your hand.

14. If you did not raise coming in with rolled up trips, when should you raise with them?

    You usually should wait to fifth or even sixth street to start playing fast.

Playing Big Pairs

1. Besides rolled up trips, what is the other hand that you should just about always play?

   A pair of aces.

2. What is the only exception?

   Against several fast players if there is a raise and many calls before the action gets to you, and your aces are dead.

3. What about kings or queens?

   Almost always play them.

4. When would you throw them away?

   You are positive that you are against a bigger pair or when your cards are dead.

5. When should you throw away a pair of tens or jacks?

   If there are several overcards still to act behind you and if your kicker is weak.

6. Example?

   You have 4♣T♠T♥ and there is a queen, a king, and an ace behind you. Normally, the correct play is to fold (unless the ante is very high).

7. When else should you throw away a big pair?

   When the pot has been raised and reraised, and both players have higher exposed cards than your pair.

8. What if there is just a raise and a call from the upcards just described?

   You should often throw your hand away.

9. Example?
   You have <u>J♥6♣</u>J♠. An ace raises and a queen calls. Unless you know these players very well (and know that there is a good chance that they do not have what they are representing), you probably should throw your hand away.

10. What is an exception to this fold?
   You have a live overcard kicker (to go along with your live pair) higher than either of the upcards of the two active players.

11. Example?
   You have <u>J♥A♣</u>J♠, there were no aces out, a queen raised, and a king reraised. You should usually play and may even want to reraise again.

12. When would your reraise be correct?
   If you feel that there is a good chance that the player with the queen will fold, and this frequently will be the case.

13. What if the player with the queen doesn't fold?
   This may require some creative play on your part to get him out of there.

14. Example?
   It may be correct to check on fourth street (if they check to you the reraiser) and then to raise on fifth street.

15. What should you do if you have a big pair, but two or more *unduplicated* upcards higher than your pair are behind you?
   You probably should fold if your kicker is poor and you don't have a two-flush.

16. What if your kicker is good?
If it is either a live overcard or a live straight flush card, and is one of your down cards, go ahead and raise. (If reraised you should usually call.)

17. If your kicker is your upcard and is the highest card on board, what should you do?
Usually raise in this spot.

18. When do you fold your big pairs after third street?
You usually should give up if one of your opponents pairs his door card or if by sixth street one of your opponents has either a four-flush or a four-straight on board.

19. How should you play a big pair?
You usually should raise or reraise and try to eliminate as many players as possible.

20. Suppose you have a big pair, but there are several players in and your hand is dead. How should you play it?
It might be best to throw it away.

21. What if your hand was live?
It would become correct to only call.

22. What is the strategic reason for only calling?
If you don't raise you will have a better chance of knocking people out on a later round.

23. Why?
The pot is smaller and there is a good chance someone else will bet. This might allow you to raise or check-raise on fourth street.

24. What if you bet out on fourth street?
    Since there is less money in the pot, your opponents will be more inclined to fold.

25. What is the second reason for only calling?
    You might reduce the odds you are getting from the pot to less than your chances of winning.

26. What if many players have limped in?
    You should often just call with a big pair and be ready to throw it away on fourth street.

27. From an early position can it be correct to "limp" with a big pair?
    Yes.

28. When would you do this?
    You might "limp" if most of the following is true:
    A. By limping you will convince most of your opponents that you do not have a big pair.
    B. Because of the cards that are showing, your big pair is even stronger than normal.
    C. You have a two-flush, and all your cards are live.
    D. A player in late position is very aggressive, and he shows a high card.
    E. Your limping in doesn't necessarily look like you are slowplaying a big hand.

29. Why do you sometimes want to play big pairs deceptively?
    You don't want to give your hand away. (This is not the same as a slowplay or a limp.)

30. Example?
    A king raised, a queen called, and you have <u>A♠A♣</u>5♦. You may only want to call in this spot.

31. When would it be correct to go ahead and reraise?
    If you have been double raising a lot with three-flushes and have been noticed.

32. When would you *definitely* reraise with this hand?
    If you think there is a possibility that you can get the initial raiser to throw his hand away.

33. Example?
    A queen raised and the king called, and the person holding the queen is a very conservative player who might throw his hand away.

34. What happens if the play doesn't work?
    That's okay. You still get more money in with the best hand.

35. When is another time that your reraise with a hand like buried aces is a must?
    In a three way pot when you think the initial raiser will reraise you to knock the third player out.

36. Another example of deceptive play?
    You are the low card with two aces in the hole, a king — someone not in a steal position — brings it in for a raise, and no one else is in the pot. You probably should just call and hope to get a raise in later.

37. What if he is in a steal position?
    Be inclined to raise. He may automatically reraise thinking that you are just defending against his possible steal.

38. What if you raise with a split big pair and a higher card behind you rereaises?
    If your kicker is higher than his upcard, you should call and be prepared to go the river.

39. What if your kicker is a live straight flush card?
    You can also call the raise. (However, if you catch blanks on fourth and fifth street you should probably give it up.)

40. Example?
    You have J♥2♣J♠. You raise, a person holding a queen reraises, and this is the kind of person who has to have at least two queens to make this play. You should now fold.

Reraising the Possible Bigger Pair

1. Is it ever correct to reraise on third street with a big pair when a higher upcard has raised?

   Yes.

2. When is this especially true?

   Against a player over whom you have good control, or against someone whose upcard is duplicated elsewhere.

3. When is this play also correct?

   Against an aggressive player who is apt to have little.

4. Example?

   An ace comes in for a raise and you have Q♦Q♣J♠. If no other queen is out and one of the three conditions mentioned above is favorable, make it two bets.

5. What if one of your queens is out?

   You still can make it two bets if your opponent is smart enough to originally raise with an ace high only, but not tricky enough to reraise without having two aces.

6. What if it now goes to three bets?

   You then can assume you are against two aces (or two kings in the hole).

7. Are there problems with reraising the ace?

   Yes.

8. What are they?
   A. There is a good chance that if you don't raise, the ace will bet into you the whole pot, which will give you a great edge if he doesn't have aces.
   B. Your opponent can always pair aces later on, even if he doesn't have them to start with.

9. What is the deciding factor?
   Is your raise required to get the pot heads-up?

10. Be specific.
    If you are in late position and there is no one between you and the ace, then the raise may not be necessary. On the other hand, if there are several players still to act behind you, a reraise is now mandatory strategy.

11. What is important to realize?
    A player who raises with an ace, without necessarily having aces, yet who does require a decent hand to make this raise, is someone you need to be concerned with.

12. Can you be more specific?
    Your opponent has a pretty good chance of either already having a pair of aces or improving to a good hand, which could be a pair of aces or better.

13. What does this mean?
    It is very dangerous to reraise someone who has an ace up if he is playing well.

14. What about reraising a possible higher pair *other* than aces?
    It is frequently clearly correct.

15. What if your kicker is higher than the pair your opponent is representing?

To *not* reraise is usually a terrible play as long as only the two of you (plus the bring-in) are in the pot to that point.

Playing Small and Medium Pairs

1. How do small pairs compare to big pairs?
   They are much worse.

2. Example?
   A deuce brings it in, and you are next with 7♣J♦7♠. *Automatically* playing this holding is a big mistake.

3. To determine whether a small or medium pair is playable when you are not in a steal position, what factors must you consider?
   A. How high your kicker is.
   B. Whether your cards are all live. (If one of your pair cards is out you should rarely play. If one of your kickers is out, it still might be worth it, but not if two of them are gone.)
   C. What the other upcards are.
   D. What the game is like.
   E. Whether your pair is in the hole. (It is usually better if the pair is in the hole, but the reverse may be true if you have an ace or a king kicker.)
   F. Whether you also have a two-card flush (or less importantly a two-card straight), especially if the flush cards are live. (Also, it is slightly better for the two-card flush to be in the hole, and it is even better if you have a two-card straight flush.)

4. What are the two most important factors?
   The size of your kicker and whether your cards are all live.

5. How high does your kicker need to be?
   Higher than any card on board (but if it isn't an ace or a king it's not that strong).

6. Example?
   A deuce brings it in. You have 3♥A♥3♠ and all your cards are live. The hand is worth playing for the bring-in.

7. What if it is a full bet?
   The hand is still worth playing.

8. Should *you* make it a full bet?
   This is debatable.

9. Should you ever reraise higher upcards?
   Yes.

10. When is this correct?
    If you can get it heads-up, your cards are live, one of their upcards is gone, or there is some chance they don't have what they are representing.

11. How long should you stay with a small or medium pair?
    This depends on what you think you have to beat, how much money is in the pot, and how the hand will be played from that point on.

12. Example?
    You have a medium pair, such as two nines. If there are no cards or only one card behind you higher than your nines, go ahead and raise, no matter what your upcard is.

13. What is another time that you should raise?
    When you have a concealed small or medium pair and the highest upcard, and you are the first one in.

14. What are the advantages of having the highest upcard with your small pair in the hole?

    It allows you to represent a different hand than what you actually have. Plus it makes it easier to make the best two pair.

15. What if you get raised and reraised?

    You should usually fold against this double bet.

16. What is the exception?

    You have a live overcard kicker (to go along with your live pair) higher than either of the upcards of the two active players.

17. What if it is raised ahead of you and you have a concealed pair lower than the upcard of the raiser?

    You should usually fold if there are any players behind you with unduplicated upcards higher than the raiser's upcard.

18. What is a reason why you should fold?

    You can be raised again.

19. What is another reason?

    Since the raiser was looking at higher upcards and still raised, he probably has a real hand.

20. Example?

    Suppose the raiser has a queen up and there is a king behind him. It is very likely that you are looking at a pair of queens, as opposed to a steal hand.

21. What will many players also have in this spot?

    A high three-flush.

22. If you have a pair and one of your pair cards is out, should you fold if it appears that someone has a higher pair?

Yes.

23. What is an exception?

If your kicker is higher than the highest card on board.

24. But even this situation is not so great unless you are holding what kicker?

An ace or a king.

25. When is the only time that a small pair, with one of the pair cards out, is automatically playable?

When you are in a good position to steal.

26. What if there are one or two higher cards behind you, but the six factors listed earlier are favorable, and no one has yet voluntarily entered the pot?

You should at least call with your pair if you have a live quality kicker.

27. Should you ever raise?

You should frequently raise whether or not your kicker is up.

28. Example?

You have 9♣J♦9♣. Your cards are live, no one is yet in the pot, but behind you is an ace and a king. (Notice that the J♦ is a straight flush card.) You should usually raise.

29. What if there are three or four cards behind you higher than your pair?

Usually fold.

30. When would you consider calling?

Only with a high kicker or if your kicker is a straight flush card that's very live on both straights and flushes.

31. If you are sure that your opponent has a big pair — such as two queens — and you have a small or medium pair, for your call to be correct what do you need (among other things)?

An ace or a king kicker.

32. Is a straight flush kicker good enough in this spot?

No, unless you are in a game with a very high ante.

33. When making this call, what else do you usually need?

Your kicker to be in the hole.

34. What is the problem if your kicker is up?

You will have to lead all the way, thus showing weakness when you check.

35. Why else is it desirable to have your kicker in the hole?

You can catch three cards to give you a hidden hand, as opposed to two cards if you have a wired pair.

36. Example?

You have 2♣A♠2♥. It is generally worth it to go all the way against a probable pair lower than aces in a heads-up situation, providing that your opponent does not improve and your cards remain live.

37. What if it is raised ahead of you, the raiser is not in a steal position, your kicker is live but small, and there are not threatening cards behind you?

You should fold.

38. When is it correct to play a small pair with a small kicker?

As an ante steal or when you know you can get in cheaply.

39. If a high card raises in front of you and you have a live pair with an even higher kicker, what should you do?

Reraise if you can get it heads-up. Otherwise, normally call.

40. What if your kicker is a straight flush card?

Call if you can anticipate a multiway pot.

41. If you raise with a medium pair, a smaller card reraises, and you know this player has a bigger pair in the hole, what should you do?

Call.

Playing Three-Flushes

1. What are four things to consider in determining how and whether to play your starting three-flush?

   A. What your position is.
   B. What your door card is.
   C. How many of your cards are out.
   D. How high your cards are.

2. If you have a three-flush and none of your suit is out, is your hand playable?

   It almost always is, unless you have three small cards and it is three bets to you, or two high cards raise and reraise.

3. Example?

   You hold 9♣2♣4♣ and no other clubs are showing. This hand is usually playable, unless one of the two exceptions just mentioned is applicable.

4. What if three or more of your suit are out?

   Your three-flush is just about always unplayable.

5. What are the exceptions?

   The hand can be played as an ante steal, or if it has value other than the three-flush aspect.

6. What can give a three-flush additional value?

   A possible straight draw or high cards.

7. Give an example of a totally worthless hand.

   You have T♦5♦2♦ and there are three diamonds out, as well as a ten and a five out.

8. If two of your suit were out, but no tens, fives, or deuces, is it worth playing?

The hand becomes barely playable as long as it doesn't cost too much.

9. When is this hand unplayable?

If you think you may be heads-up against a high pair.

10. If your cards are completely live, you are *heads-up* against a raiser, and your three-flush contains all small cards, should you fold?

You might want to fold, especially if you are against a good player.

11. But what if the raiser may not have anything?

It is clearly at least a call.

12. What if almost all the tens, fives, and deuces are gone, but your flush cards are completely live?

You usually should play in a *multiway* pot.

13. You are the first one in and you have a three-flush with a high card showing. What do you do?

You should usually, but not always, enter the pot with a raise.

14. Suppose you hold a big straight flush draw such as A♠K♠J♠. How should you play?

You probably want to raise so that you can narrow the field in case you make a high pair.

15. What if you don't raise, or if you can't thin the field?

Having a lot of opponents when you hold this hand is also good.

16. Suppose you have a high three-flush with straight flush potential. How do you play if you are first one in?

Normally raise only if there is no more than one card higher behind you.

17. What about a small three-card straight flush?

You should not raise unless a few players are already in.

18. What if you have a three-flush with one card higher than the raiser's door card?

Then you should always at least call, unless your hand is not very live.

19. If you have a three-flush, and two big cards ahead of you raise and reraise, when can you play?

You can play only if you have at least one card higher than the two big cards.

20. Example?

A ten raises, a queen reraises, and you have K♣2♣J♣. Since you hold a king, go ahead and play as long as your cards are live.

21. Suppose there is just a raise and a call?

Then you can play any three-flush if your cards are live.

22. What if your three-flush is small and two of your suit are out?

You usually should throw your hand away.

23. Suppose someone has just called the bring-in. When is it correct to raise with a three-flush?

When you have two overcards and at least a medium card up.

24. What if you only have one overcard?

It may be right to raise, particularly if it is an ace or a king.

25. Example?

You have K♥Q♥8♥ and someone has limped in with a ten up.

26. What if the Q♥ was a small heart instead?

It still might be correct to raise in an attempt to get heads-up.

27. What if someone has already raised, you have two overcards, and one of them is up?

You can go ahead and reraise.

Playing Three-Straights

1. When deciding whether to play a three-straight, what eight factors do you consider?

   A. How high your cards are.
   B. How live your straight cards are.
   C. How live your pair cards are.
   D. Whether you have a two-flush.
   E. The other cards on board.
   F. Who is already playing.
   G. How much it is to you, that is, whether you can play for the bring-in, one bet, or two bets.
   H. The ability of your opponents.

2. Is it ever worth calling one full bet, but not two full bets, cold?

   Yes.

3. Example?

   You have 8♣9♠10♥. One seven and one queen are out, but no jacks or sixes are gone. Now the queen raises and an ace calls. Go ahead and call for a full bet.

4. What if the ace had reraised?

   You should throw the hand away.

5. Is this hand as good as it appears?

   No.

6. Why?

   It looks as though *two* queens are out. So if you catch a jack, you now have just five straight cards left.

7. Can a three-straight be played for two cold bets?

   Occasionally.

8. When does this occur?

When the conditions outlined are favorable and particularly if you have high cards (overcards to your opponents' probable pairs) and/or a two-flush.

9. When you have close decisions with hands like straight draws, what should you keep in mind?

How well your opponents play.

10. Example?

If your opponent is the type of player who gets "married" to a high pair, you know that if you make your hand you will get paid off all the way, even if it is obvious that you have a made straight.

11. When is it correct to play a small three-card "gut-shot" straight, such as 9♣7♥6♦?

The main thing to consider is how live your cards are (especially the eight in this case). Also, be more inclined to play if everyone else has small cards and you have an overcard.

12. What about three-straights with *two* gaps?

They generally should not be played at all.

13. What is the problem with gaps?

Unless your cards are high, you must catch that specific "gut" card.

14. Example?

You have T♣9♥7♦. You must catch an eight. But if you are holding 9♥8♦7♣ there is no specific card that you must catch.

15. What if your gut shot is bigger, such as Q♠T♥9♦?
    You should be somewhat more inclined to play, since your straight, and more importantly your pairs, will probably be bigger.

16. If you have a consecutive three-straight, but three of your cards are dead, should you play?
    You definitely should not play unless you have a good chance to steal the antes.

17. What if two of your straight cards are dead?
    You probably should not play, especially if other considerations (such as how high your cards are) appear unfavorable.

18. What else should you consider?
    If a card you need is shown by someone who has stayed in on third street, it is likely that he has additional cards you need.

19. If an opponent just calls the bring-in, is it okay to raise with your three-straight?
    If you have at least two cards higher than his upcard, and there is no more than one higher card behind you, then it is okay to raise with your three-straight.

20. Is it ever correct to reraise with a three-straight?
    It is rarely correct to do so.

21. Are there exceptions?
    Yes. One exception is covered in the section on "Playing Big Cards Against a Medium Pair" on page 113. Another time to reraise occurs when you think the original raiser may be semi-bluffing.

22. When should you play three-straights made up of small cards?

They generally should only be played when you can get in cheaply and when your hand is live, or when you have a chance to steal the antes.

More Discussion on Calling Versus Raising

1. Suppose three players call, and you are last. What should you do?

    Call liberally.

2. Should you raise with many hands?

    No.

3. Why?

    You are only getting 3-to-1 on your raise.

4. If a deuce brings it in, three people call the bring-in, and you are last, how often should you limp if you don't fold?

    At least two-thirds of the time.

5. What will the typical pro do?

    Raise two-thirds of the time if he plays his hand.

6. Why is he wrong?

    He cannot stop players from coming in behind him since he is already last.

7. Example?

    A deuce brings it in, a five calls, a seven calls, and a nine calls. You have Q♣8♦Q♠ and are next to the bring-in. You should just call.

8. If instead of the 8♦ your kicker was the J♠, what should you do?

    You could go ahead and raise.

9. Why?

Your hand plays much better multiway.

10. What if the pot is not multiway and you are not last to act?

You should generally raise with more hands than most people do.

11. If you hold 5♥T♦5♣ and there is a player with a nine up behind you, why is it better to make it a full bet and have him reraise you than it would be to just call and have him make it a full bet?

This may allow callers behind him, and you now have to play multiway.

12. Are we saying that you should call with 5♥T♦5♣ if a nine raises?

No. You should frequently fold.

13. What are we saying?

You should make the original raise yourself if your biggest fear would be a reraise from a nine showing.

14. Suppose an ace raises, you have 5♥5♦K♠, and you think the ace may be stealing. How should you play?

You may be better off reraising in an attempt to limit the pot to the two of you.

15. Suppose there is a queen behind you?

It is important to knock him out if he has two queens because the ace might be bluffing.

16. Now suppose in this situation your hand was 5♥K♦K♠. Is it important to knock someone out?

No.

17. Why?

If your opponent has aces you still have to make at least two pair to win.

18. How does this affect the player with the queens?

He will have to catch a third one to beat you.

19. What should influence your decision of whether to take it to two full bets?

Your position.

20. Example?

If a queen raises, a jack calls, and you are next with a pair of kings, you should reraise to get everyone out behind you. But if you were last, you are probably better off just calling.

21. If you hold a hand that does much better heads-up than multiway, what should you do?

You should try to get heads-up if possible.

22. If you can't get it heads-up what should you decide?

Whether to call or to fold.

23. What do typical players do?

They will call when the expert raises, and they will call when the expert folds.

24. What hands do you want to play heads-up?

Pairs, high cards without pairs, and high straight draws.

25. If you have a hand that's much better off multiway than heads-up against an overcard, what should you do in early position?

Limp in.

26. Example?

    You have 5♠2♠T♠. There is an ace and a king behind you and a lot of low cards behind them.

27. What is another time when you want to limp up front?

    You have a hand that prefers to get in as cheaply as possible because you are willing to give it up on fourth street if you don't catch a perfect card.

28. Example?

    A three-card-straight or a three-card-flush when a couple of your cards are out.

More Discussion on Playable Hands

1. What must you take into account?
   The cards that are out.

2. Example?
   If a queen raises and another queen calls, you should be very inclined to play against them.

3. In addition to how live your hand is, what else should you consider?
   How the other upcards may impact your opponents' hands.

4. Example?
   A deuce brings it in, a trey folds, a nine calls, another nine calls, you're next with 9♣3♦9♠, and behind you are an eight and two sixes. You should fold.

5. Another example?
   You have 5♥6♦5♦. You are against someone who holds a pair of aces, and one of the remaining aces as well as one of the remaining aces' kicker is out. Your hand is playable heads-up.

6. If you have live cards and your opponent has a dead card to his big pair, is it correct for you to play heads-up with a small pair and a straight flush card?
   Yes.

7. What about this same hand in a three-way pot?
   It becomes a disaster.

8. Why?

If you make two pair you will frequently beat the player with the big pair, but lose to the third player.

9. What does this mean?

You should frequently reraise in this spot if you believe that the extra bet will get the pot heads-up.

10. What is the problem with playing a hand like 5♥Q♦5♠ multiway?

Your chances of winning are going down faster than the size of the pot is going up.

11. Why is that?

A large part of your profit comes form winning with two small pair. This contribution disappears once it becomes multiway.

12. What must you do at the beginning of every hand?

Look at your three cards and decide if your hand has been helped or hurt by the cards that are out. You must also take into account how many players you are likely to be up against.

13. Example?

If you have 9♥7♥4♥ all you normally do is see how many other hearts are in the other players' hands.

14. What if you have a medium high three-straight?

You need to consider what the upcards are, whether your cards are dead, how many people you will be up against, whether their cards are dead, will hitting a pair figure to win, what will happen on the next round, and who will act first on the next round.

Randomizing Your Play

1. What can the cards that are out or the number of players in the pot help you do?

   Something other than what appears to be normal.

2. What three things result when you just call with a pair of kings when one of the kings is up?

   A. Most players won't put you on that hand as it is being played.
   B. Once your hand is exposed, all but the best players will think that you were trying to be tricky.
   C. When you call in some other spot with a king up, your opponents will worry that you have kings.

3. What does this accomplish for you?

   You will get randomness without actually having to be random.

Playing Weak Hands

1. Do many players get out of line on third street?

Yes.

2. Example?

Suppose you start with <u>T♠T♥</u>8♦. An ace raises, a king calls, and you call. You should have folded.

3. Assuming that you incorrectly called, suppose that on fourth street the ace catches a jack, the king catches a ten, and you catch a seven. Is it correct to call again?

No, you have caught only enough to "suck you in."

4. What if the third street bet is only the bring-in and it is unlikely that you will be raised?

Things are a little different. In fact, many good players probably play a little too tight in this spot.

5. If you do play a weak hand for the bring-in and are raised, what should you do?

Usually fold and save the rest of the bet.

6. Why should you fold when raised?

There are two reasons for this:

A. It's costing you more money.

B. The fact that the pot has been raised has diminished the value of your hand.

7. If you are in a game where people frequently limp for the bring-in, should you often limp in behind them?

Yes, especially if the players are weak.

8. What are you hoping for?

To catch a perfect card on fourth street.

9. What if you don't catch what you want?

You must be prepared to fold.

10. Example?

If you are holding K♥J♣9♦, and the queens and tens are live, you should frequently call the bring-in. Also consider the kings, jacks, and nines.

11. If you catch a queen or ten on fourth street (giving you a gut shot) how long do you stay with the hand?

It depends on whether you have seen any of your other straight cards, as well as the other kings, jacks, and nines; how much money is in the pot; what you think you must beat; and how you think the hand will be played.

12. Why is "how the hand will be played" important?

It gives you an idea of how much you can win if you make your hand and what it will cost you if you don't.

13. What else does calling the bring-in allow you to do?

Punish people who don't raise enough.

14. Example?

If two or three people are in and you have a hand like A♥K♥8♠ or A♠K♦4♠ you should call if your cards are live.

15. When is this an especially good play?

Against a player who will pay you off all the way if you make your hand.

16. What must you take into account when making these calls?
    Whether your hand has the potential to improve enough that it would be a mistake for your opponent to pay off all the way.

17. What if it is a full bet?
    It wouldn't hurt to abstain from calling with weak hands.

Playing Extra Hands Heads-Up

1. What type of player should you play many hands against?
   Someone who plays badly, plays too loose, can be easily manipulated, or you can easily read.

2. Example?
   A player with an eight raises, you have T♥8♦7♣ and think that he only has a pair of eights.

3. What should you notice?
   There are many cards that you can catch that will scare him. This includes all cards above an eight. In addition, you know that one of his eights is out.

4. What if it comes out badly on the next card?
   You should fold.

5. What if it comes out good?
   You can become the aggressor.

6. What if someone else has called?
   You should throw this hand away.

Heads-Up Versus Multiway

1. What is the main thing to remember as the number of hands increases?

Certain hands go down in value.

2. Give an example of a hand that loses value in a multiway pot?

T♦3♥T♠

3. What hands are better heads-up?

Big pairs.

4. What hands are better multiway?

The drawing hands.

5. What does this mean?

You should raise or reraise with big pairs, unless your raise is unlikely to thin out the field.

6. Example?

If a jack raises, everyone calls, and you are last with K♦4♣K♠, it may be better to just call and see what develops.

7. What is the problem with reraising in this situation?

You make the pot so large that your opponents who otherwise would play badly by calling from fourth street on are now playing correctly.

8. Anything else?

Not reraising also disguises your hand so that it is easier to thin out the field later. In addition, it introduces an element of randomization to your play.

9. What is the exception?

You still should raise for value if your hand is extremely strong and completely live.

10. How should you play if you have a big pair and only a small number of people are in?

You should just about always raise (or reraise).

11. Should you ever reraise in a multiway pot with a small pair?

Yes.

12. Example?

You are low with 3♥A♦3♣. Five people call your bring-in, and then a jack raises. You usually should reraise.

13. What is the reason that your reraise is a better play than either calling or folding?

First, you most likely will knock out everyone but the jack. Second, the pot is large enough that folding is wrong. And third, the hand plays better heads-up against a probable pair of jacks.

14. Should you now be prepared to go to the river?

Yes, unless your opponent pairs jacks on board.

Fourth Street

1. If you think you have the best hand on fourth street, what should you try to do?

Eliminate players.

2. Example?

After receiving your second upcard you have what you believe is the best hand, are first to act in a three-person pot, think the second player is weak, and are sure that the third player will bet. Your play is now to try for a check-raise.

3. Example?

You limp in with <u>K♥8♥</u>6♥, are called by the 7♣, and are raised by the Q♠ (meaning a probable pair of queens). If you catch a king on the next round, and your two opponents catch seemingly non-threatening cards, you should try for a check-raise if the probable pair of queens is last to act.

4. Is trying for the check-raise sometimes wrong?

This could be true if you raised coming in on third street or if you catch a scare card on fourth street. Your threatening board may cause the last player to check.

5. What else should you keep in mind when trying to make this play?

The opponent on the end needs to be an aggressive player.

6. What else is important to big pair play on fourth street?

To add deception.

7. What happens when you bet?

You are telling your opponent that you most likely have a big pair (unless your opponent's board is weak, in which case your bet becomes somewhat automatic).

8. What if you check in this situation and your opponent bets?

You should occasionally flat-call. However, it is usually best to raise.

9. What will the raise accomplish?

It will not only get more money into the pot immediately, but also may psychologically commit your opponent to go all the way, even if you catch cards that indicate he should get out.

10. What is the main problem with just calling?

You will be first to act on fifth street, and if you check again your opponent may now check behind you.

11. Suppose you have a fairly good hand and your opponent catches a suited card that goes well with his medium upcard. If you are high, what should you do?

Consider checking.

12. Why?

There is a good chance that your opponent will bet. He either has a good draw or is likely to represent one.

13. Example?

You have K♥K♦6♣Q♠. Your opponent started with the 8♥ and catches the 9♥. You usually should check and call.

14. If a good player calls on third street against a possible steal raise and it is checked to him on fourth street, will he bet?

Usually.

15. What does this mean?

    If you raise in a steal position on third street with, let's say, a king up, are called, then catch a complete blank on fourth street, and your opponent catches something even mildly scary, you almost always should check, whether you have a hand or not.

16. Can you steal a lot on fourth street?

    No.

17. Suppose you have a hand like <u>J♣9♦</u>J♠4♥, and are facing a bet from something like ace-queen suited. Do you call?

    No. You usually should throw your hand away. This would be correct even if your kickers were better.

18. What hands should you call with?

    Those holdings that can improve to very large hands, specifically hands that can beat aces up.

19. If your opponent catches an ace on fourth street, is this dangerous?

    Yes.

20. Why?

    Because many players call with high cards or a small pair and an ace kicker, especially if there was no raise on third street, and even if your opponent hasn't paired his ace, he may pair it down the road.

Pairing Your Door Card on Fourth Street

1. What are your options when you pair your door card on fourth street?

   You can make either a single or maximum bet (or check).

2. Are there any situations when you pair your door card on fourth street where making the single bet is correct?

   Yes, there are three distinct situations.

3. Suppose you have made three-of-a-kind or a higher two pair than your opponent can have. For example, you pair sevens and have kings in the hole, while he shows jack-five offsuit. What should you do?

   This probably is one of those times when you should bet the minimum.

4. When do these times occur?

   When you are quite sure that a maximum bet will cause your opponent to fold, but you don't want him to fold even for half a bet.

5. Explain this further.

   If your opponent will make a mistake by calling you for half a bet, why not make that bet instead of a maximum bet that will force him to (correctly) throw his hand away.

6. When is another time that you usually should make half a bet?

   When you have only one pair and are convinced that if you are beaten you will be called for either a big bet or small bet, and if you are not, your opponent will fold for either a big bet or a small bet.

7. What else may happen?

   The more observant players might fold even when you are beaten, since you also are sometimes betting the lesser amount when you have made trips.

8. Example?

   A weak player showing the 3♦ brings it in. You start off with J♥4♥7♥ and just call. Everyone else folds. Your opponent catches an offsuit queen, and you make open sevens. You should bet the minimum, not the maximum.

9. Why is the minimum bet correct?

   If your opponent has queens, he will call for either the minimum or the maximum, but if he does not have queens, he should fold for just the single bet.

10. What if you bet the minimum and your opponent does call?

    Then you should assume that he has queens.

11. Is this single bet still correct if you are not heads-up?

    Yes. Any time you are sure that your opponents will fold for a full bet, you should consider betting the minimum instead of the maximum.

12. When does this play typically come up?

    Against weak players, particularly tourists, who can't resist a bargain.

13. When you make trips, why should you not always bet the minimum?

    If you become known as someone who often makes this play, observant opponents will realize that when you do bet the maximum, you probably don't have three-of-a-kind.

14. In a multiway pot if you think there is a chance that someone will call the maximum (and you have made trips) what is your best play?

Bet the maximum even if his upcards look weak.

15. What is the third time to bet just the minimum?

You don't have much, and you think you are beat and will be called if you bet. However, you also believe that if you check, your opponent will bet the maximum and you would consider calling his bet.

16. Example?

You call with 2♥3♥7♥, are raised by a jack, and are fairly sure that you are against a pair of jacks. Now you make open sevens.

17. When should you bet the maximum in this spot?

If you think your opponent will fold.

18. Is this likely?

Usually not.

19. Why is that?

Many players automatically will call if they have a big pair or a big draw.

20. For the minimum bet to be correct, what criterion must be established?

Your opponent must be likely to bet the maximum if you check.

21. Example?
    You are low with 9♥2♣2♠. Nobody raises. Now you pair your door card, giving you trips. If the last deuce is out, and you are against four or five other people, you probably should check. Notice that you would certainly check if you had only two deuces.

22. Should you raise immediately on fourth street?
    Yes.

23. Why is that?
    Because just calling tends to give your hand away anyway.

24. What's another benefit of check-raising early?
    It may make an opponent fold, which means he won't get a fifth-street card to beat you.

25. Suppose you make four-of-a-kind on fourth street. Should you check?
    Yes, no matter how obvious it is.

26. What is the standard advice?
    Check against terrible players, but to bet against good players because they won't be fooled.

27. Why is this probably wrong?
    Even good players don't have the psychological strength to fold a full house against one pair showing on fifth street, even if they are almost sure that they are against quads.

28. Example?
    A bunch of small cards call the bring-in, you have A♠A♦A♣, and you raise. On fourth street, you catch the A♥ and your opponents catch nothing special. You should check.

29. What will happen if you bet on fourth street?
    Anyone with two pair will fold.

Fifth Street

1. The decision on fifth street is a close second in importance to the decision on third street. Why is that?

    Because this is when the bets double in size and a call usually ties you on to the end, which may mean putting in an additional two or more large bets, especially in an aggressive game.

2. Suppose you have a hand, such as a flush draw, and you will at least call a bet. Do you bet it?

    You should always bet this hand if some reasonable chance exists that your opponent will fold.

3. Example?

    Your opponent has caught two blanks, and from the way the hand has been played, you suspect that he started with a three-flush or a small pair.

4. When should you check?

    When you know your opponent will always check behind you — and you want this — and you are absolutely certain you will be called if you bet. However, it still may be better to bet to set up a steal on a subsequent round.

5. If you have a drawing hand on fifth street, do you want to keep as many players in as possible?

    Not necessarily. If your drawing hand can make a big pair that might win against one opponent, you may want to raise. (Or if you already have a pair, you may want to raise to limit the pot to two players.)

6. If you have a choice of playing against either one opponent or two opponents, why is it often better to be heads-up?

   You may win with a bigger pair or two small pair. Moreover, in a two-person pot, your opponent may not bet if you catch a big card.

7. When else is it correct to raise on fifth street with a drawing hand?

   When many players are in, you are in a late position, and you think you have the *best* drawing hand.

8. What else is important on fifth street?

   To eliminate players when you believe you have the best hand. In other words, almost never give a free card.

9. What if you are against many opponents and only have one big pair?

   You should usually check, even if it seems like you have the best hand.

10. Why?

    There is a good chance that everyone will call, and you will be a bigger dog than the number of bets that you are collecting.

11. What is another fifth-street concept that concerns raising?

    To recognize those times you should raise when you are almost certain that you do *not* have the best hand.

12. Example?

A player who has just caught an offsuit ace checks. The next player has ? ? 10♣4♥8♦ and bets. You have two queens and a three-flush, and your cards are live. It is a multiway pot. There is a person behind you who you suspect has two kings and you think the bettor started with a pair of tens and probably has made two pair. The correct play is to raise to drive out the other hands. This play notably increases your chances of winning (though you are still a small underdog) because you are now more likely to win if you improve your hand.

13. What should you do on sixth street in the situation just described?

Bet if you improve; otherwise, it is usually best to check.

14. In general, is trying for a check-raise on fifth street good strategy?

No. Your check may cause you to lose a double-size bet. You need to be very sure that your opponent will bet. Also, your check may allow a miracle card to beat you.

15. What if you pair your door card?

It usually will stop your opponent from betting.

16. When is the time to attempt a check-raise on fifth street?

With concealed trips or sometimes a high two pair.

17. What if your fifth-street card is the same suit as your door card, but you actually have hidden trips?

You usually should bet and try to represent a flush draw.

18. When would you definitely not try for a check-raise on fifth street?

When you are against weak, timid players, because they do not bet often enough.

19. Can a check-raise on fifth street get you a free card?
    It might.

20. What is the play?
    To represent a strong hand in such a manner that if you miss on sixth street, your opponent will not bet (after you check).

21. Example?
    You raise on third street with a T♠A♣T♥, and are reraised by a queen, meaning at least a pair of queens. On fourth street you both catch blanks. He bets and you call. On fifth street, you catch a king versus another blank for your opponent. Check-raise a weak player.

22. What can happen on sixth street in this example?
    If you catch an ace, you get an extra bet. If you catch a king, your opponent will fold, which you won't like, but at least you got more money in the pot. And if you pair your fourth-street card, your opponent probably will fold, and you want him to do so.

23. Should you call on fifth street with a small pair and a three-flush?
    Neither calling nor folding is automatic.

24. What must you consider?
    What you think you have to beat, how much money is in the pot, and how the hand will be played from that point on. If most of these are favorable, you should call.

25. When else should you call on fifth street with a small pair?
    If you have either an ace or two overcards to your opponent's probable pair, and if your cards are live.

Sixth Street

1. Sometimes on sixth street you find yourself in a situation where you are either a small favorite or a huge underdog, but you don't know which. How should this hand be played?

It is best to check and call.

2. Example?

You have a big pair and are probably against a smaller pair, but you could also be against a flush.

3. If you do bet on sixth street, should you expect to be called?

Yes, even weak hands almost always will stay with you unless your board is extremely scary. But they probably will bet in these spots if you check, so you get the same amount of money in the pot without risking a raise.

4. What is a common sixth-street mistake?

Not raising when a raise may knock out a third player who might beat you.

5. Will you expand on this?

Failing to raise can cost you the pot by allowing a weak hand to get good enough pot odds to call and outdraw you.

6. Should you ever try for a check-raise on sixth street?

Yes, when you are fairly sure you have the best hand and are against an aggressive player who likes to bet medium and big pairs.

7. What else might your check-raise accomplish?

It may make your opponent throw his hand away (although this is an unlikely event).

8. Example?

You have a hidden high two pair or hidden trips, but your first two cards were suited. You bet on fourth and fifth streets, but have caught apparent blanks on fifth and sixth streets. Against an aggressive opponent, who you believe has a good pair and will put you on a four-flush, you can try for a check-raise.

9. When is trying for a check-raise in this situation wrong?

Against a timid player who might not bet.

10. What is an even more creative play (against tough players only) that you occasionally can make?

You have paired your door card on fourth street and have made trips. If your opponent has called your fourth- and fifth-street bets, he doesn't think you have three-of-a-kind, and you therefore can check-raise on sixth street.

11. What if you are not sure about trying for a check-raise?

It is best to go ahead and bet.

12. Why is that?

First, you may lose a bet by checking, and second, there may be some chance that your opponent will fold, which means he can't get a free card to beat you.

Seventh Street

1. Suppose that going into seventh street you have an obvious pair of aces, and your opponent has an obvious pair of kings. What are your options if you improve down the river?

   To bet, to try for a check-raise, or to check with the intention of calling if your opponent bets.

2. If you don't improve, what are your options?

   To bet, hoping that one pair will call; to check with the intention of calling, hoping to catch a steal; to check with the intention of raising, hoping to make two pair fold; or to check with the intention of folding.

3. When is betting a pair of aces or aces up, hoping that one pair will call, usually the best play?

   When your opponent's cards are slightly dead.

4. Is automatically betting aces up and checking a pair of aces correct?

   No.

5. If you think your opponent will call 100 percent of the time when he does not improve, what is the correct play?

   Bet both aces and aces up (and three aces).

6. If you think your opponent will always bet if he has made kings up or three kings, what should you do?

   Check, unless he almost always will call with just two kings.

7. Why is that?

   You don't lose anything when he has kings up and you have aces up.

8. If you think your opponent usually will check two kings (and sometimes fold if you bet), but will bet kings up or better — and, assuming that he does bet, call if you check-raise — what should you do?

    You should check aces with the intention of folding and check aces up with the intention of raising.

9. If you think he will bet only kings up or better but *fold* kings up if you check-raise, what should you do?

    Your correct strategy is to now check and call with aces up (since he might have three kings), but to check-raise with two aces to make him fold kings up!

10. When making this play, is there anything else that you should consider?

    Yes, a typical player is more likely to fold a hand like jacks up rather than kings up.

11. Suppose you have made two pair on the end, such as queens up, your opponent bets, and he has been representing a pair of kings all along. What should you do?

    Normally this is an automatic call.

12. What if you're against a very timid and readable opponent who never bets one pair for value when all the cards are out?

    You probably should fold.

13. What if you're against a very aggressive player who almost always will bet kings for value?

    It may be correct to raise with queens up.

14. When can you profitably make this play?

    If your opponent's upcards are dead *and* you think he will call your raise with just one pair (or might fold a higher two pair).

15. When you have made a big two pair, what should you consider when determining whether to bet?

   How concealed your hand is.

16. Example?

   If you have kings over fours, you would prefer that neither pair is showing, especially the kings.

17. What should you keep in mind on seventh street?

   Most players will call if you bet, and also will call if you raise or check-raise.

18. Should raising on the end as a bluff be done very often?

   No, only rarely.

19. When might this be correct?

   Against an opponent who will bet a mediocre hand for value on the end, but who also is willing to throw his hand away if raised.

20. When is another time?

   In a three-way pot to knock out the winner.

21. If you are caught raising without a hand, should you try it again?

   It might be correct to try it again if your opponent thinks you won't do it more than once.

22. Would you ever lay down a decent hand on the end?

   Rarely. However, if you know a player extremely well, you can make some laydowns that normally would be wrong. But your judgement must be accurate.

23. Is it sometimes possible to get three bets on the end?

   Yes, against an aggressive player.

24. Example?

You have made a full house and believe that your opponent has been trying for a flush. If he makes his hand and you bet, you can then reraise after he raises.

25. What else can happen?

Your opponent might miss his flush, but still may make something, such as a high pair, and call.

26. What if your opponent is the timid type?

It is probably better to try for a check-raise.

27. Should you usually call on seventh street?

Yes.

28. Why?

Because the pots get so big.

29. When might it be correct to throw your hand away?

If you face the threat of a raise from a third player.

30. What is the biggest mistake you can make mathematically?

To throw away the best hand when the pot is large.

31. What about calling on the end with a hand that you should not have called with?

This can never be a big mistake.

32. What is another reason for calling on the end?

To prevent players from bluffing you in the future.

33. Suppose your opponent who has been high all the way and has been checking to you, suddenly bets on the river?

You should never fold (unless you have absolutely nothing) if this player has shown that he will bluff in this situation.

34. When is another time that you should call a surprise bet?

When it appears that you may have been bluffing up to that point.

35. Example?

Suppose you started with two aces, one of which was up, and another ace was out. If your opponent caught an ace on fifth or sixth street and bets into you on the river, he may be bluffing since he will think you don't have what you are representing.

36. What about not betting for value on the end?

It can't be a big mistake since you have cost yourself mathematically only a fraction of a bet. But these fractions add up.

37. What about not raising when you should raise?

This can be a disaster if it allows a third player to overcall and beat you. But heads-up, you again are costing yourself only a fraction of a bet when you miss a raise, therefore it is not so terrible. On the other hand, if you are fairly sure that your raise will be called by a worse hand, you eventually will cost yourself a lot of money by not raising in these spots.

38. If your opponent has a pair on board (not involving his door card) and he bets, should you raise if you have made a straight or a flush?

It depends on your opponent. If it looks as though you have a four-flush and you are still bet into, you could have a problem.

39. What will a good player do when he is looking at a possible straight or flush draw?

He often will bet if he thinks it is likely for you to have only a pair.

40. What if a weak or scared player bets?
    Be more concerned.

41. Can you occasionally bluff on seventh street?
    Yes, especially when you have a four-flush showing, but have absolutely nothing and are pretty sure that your opponent is trying for a higher flush.

42. When else can you sometimes bluff?
    If your opponent has a pair showing that does not involve his door card, you can bet at a player who is capable of laying down two pair.

Defending Against the Possible Ante Steal

1. Suppose a late-position player raises and you think he might not have much. What should you do?

   If you think this player will frequently fold a lot of his hands, you can reraise with virtually anything.

2. Are there many players who play this way?

   No.

3. What if you think your opponent probably has little but will call your raise?

   One option is to just call and bet into him on fourth street if you fall high and he catches bad.

4. What if he catches good?

   Be prepared to fold if your hand is weak.

5. What if his upcard is larger than yours and you have next to nothing?

   The correct play usually is to fold unless you are sure that you can maneuver your opponent as just described.

6. What if you have a small pair and a weak upcard, and you are last to act?

   You should call against someone who is on a likely steal. Remember, most stealers will call a reraise if you have a small card showing.

7. What if your pair is a little larger?

   You can consider reraising against a possible steal.

8. How often should you reraise?

About half the time (with your better hands) in this situation.

9. What else should you consider?

The rank of your opponent's upcard. The lower it is, the more inclined to reraise you should be.

10. Example?

Against an ace, rarely reraise; against an eight, reraise much more often.

11. If you are the bring-in, when can you call a raise with two big cards in the hole?

You can call if the raiser does not have an ace or a king up if you have two big cards (higher than his upcard) in the hole.

12. What if your upcard is very low?

It may be better to just throw your hand away.

13. Example?

You have K♦J♥6♠. A player in a steal position with a 9♣ up raises, no one else is yet in the pot, and you know that he will raise with anything. You normally can go ahead and call. If your opponent's upcard is a queen or higher, you should fold. You also might fold with a smaller upcard.

14. What if you feel that your opponent requires some sort of hand?

Then this call is too loose.

Playing Two Pair Against a Hidden Big Pair

1. If you raise on third street with a small or medium pair and are reraised by an obvious big pair *in the hole*, we stated that you should call. Why?

   Except for the last card, your opponent cannot make two pair without you knowing it.

2. What if your opponent reraised with a big card up?

   You usually would not know if (or when) he makes two pair.

3. If you know your opponent has a big pair in the hole, how should you play your pair?

   You should call all the way to the end, as long as he hasn't paired his board. If you make two hidden pair you should raise (or check-raise) but usually not until sixth street.

4. Why do you usually wait until sixth street to raise with your two hidden pair?

   No matter when you raise, your opponent will not fold his big pair. You will be able to get only one raise in, so you may as well wait to make sure that your opponent does not draw out on you. For instance, if you raise on fourth street and your opponent makes an open pair on fifth street, you will wish you had not done it.

5. When would it be correct to raise before sixth street?

   When your board develops "kind of scary," such as a three-straight or three-flush on fifth street.

6. When is another time?
   Against a timid opponent who might check on sixth street even though he would have no reason to believe that his pair of kings or aces is not the best hand.

7. What is the general concept?
   If an opponent is betting into you, and you figure your hand is better and you have only one chance for a raise, you should wait until sixth street to get this raise in.

8. What else can happen if you raise earlier?
   If you make an open pair that fills you up, your earlier raise is likely to cause your oppponent to fold, and you don't want him to fold.

9. Does this concept apply to multiway pots?
   No.

10. What if the pot is multiway?
    You should try to run out as many opponents as possible, as soon as possible.

11. Suppose you have paired your door card on fourth street and have two small pair?
    Bet the maximum into your opponent and hope he throws his hand away.

12. What if your opponent calls?
    Continue to bet unless you have a good reason not to.

13. What could be a good reason to check?
    Your opponent makes an open pair.

Playing Against a Paired Door Card (on the Early Rounds)

1. What do you do most of the time when your opponent pairs his door card?

   Fold.

2. When is this particularly true?

   On fourth or fifth street when the pot is not yet too large.

3. What is the most important exception to folding?

   Your opponent is a wild, loose player who plays almost any three cards, plus you can beat his pair.

4. Are there other exceptions?

   Yes.

5. Describe them.

   A. The low card brought it in, did not have to call a raise, and now pairs his door card.

   B. A lower card raised earlier, you are very sure he has a big pair in the hole, and you have a hand that either:

      1. Can beat his likely two pair.
      2. Contains a higher pair than what you think he has in the hole, and the pot is large, or
      3. Is a live four-card draw.

6. When else can you also play?

   If you doubt that you are up against trips and you have two bigger pair than your opponent's open pair, such as nines and eights versus sevens showing. It is better for both of your pairs to be higher than his open pair so that if he does have trips and fills up, your potential full house will always beat him.

7. If someone with a low card who was not the bring-in, but who called a raise on third street, pairs his door card, should you usually fold?

   Yes.

8. Example?

   If someone limps in with a seven up, calls a raise, and catches a seven, you usually should throw your hand away.

9. What if you have any doubts about what you should do when your opponent pairs his door card on fourth street?

   Fold.

10. What if someone pairs his door card on a later street?

    Be more inclined to call, but only because the pot is bigger.

11. When is one time that you should be more inclined to call?

    If one of your opponent's trip cards is dead.

12. Example?

    On third street your opponent has the 7♣ as his door card, and there were three other clubs out. Now it is more likely that he has trips if he pairs his door card. However, if no clubs were out, he is more likely to have started with a flush draw. If no clubs were out *and* a seven was dead, you would be inclined to continue playing even if he makes open sevens on fourth street.

13. If your opponent is a weak player who had the second highest upcard and did not enter the pot with a raise, is he likely to have three-of-a-kind if he pairs his door card?

He may be less likely.

14. When would this be particularly true?

If he was the first one to voluntarily enter the pot and the player who holds the highest card acts after him.

Continuing with a Draw

1. If you catch a fourth suited card on fourth street, should you be prepared to go all the way?

   Usually.

2. What if you don't catch a fourth suited card on fourth street?

   You still should call about 60 percent of the time.

3. What should you call with?

   Call on fourth street if you have any kind of improvement or if other conditions are favorable.

4. Be specific.

   Call if you made a pair; if your cards are live; if your cards are high; if you have straight possibilities, or if you are getting big odds.

5. Example?

   If you catch an offsuit king to go along with a small three-flush, you usually should call because you now may be able to win the pot by pairing kings.

6. What if you think you are against aces?

   You should fold.

7. What if you make a four-flush on fourth street?

   Usually bet or raise, and be prepared to see the river card.

8. When would you abandon a four-flush?

   When one of your oppoentns makes something extremely threatening, like two pair or three-of-a-kind on board.

9. When is another time you should abandon a four-flush?
When one of your opponents pairs his door card and his play strongly indicates trips.

10. What if the pot is extremely large?
It is correct to call.

11. What if you make a large pair on fourth street or beyond to go along with your draw?
The pair is now the main consideration to your strategy.

12. What about straight draws?
Much of what is appropriate for flush draws also applies to straight draws.

13. If you don't improve to a four-straight, how long do you stay with the hand?
It depends on what you think you have to beat, how much money is in the pot, and how the hand will be played from that point on.

14. What if you start with a three-straight and catch a blank?
Be less likely to call than you would be if you started with a three-flush.

15. How do you play a four-straight?
It depends on the situation. Sometimes call, but sometimes raise.

Playing a Big Pair Against a Possible Flush or Straight

1. Is it ever best to check and call with a big pair on fifth street?
   Yes.

2. When would this be correct?
   Against a three-flush showing or a hand like ? ? 6♥7♦8♠.

3. Why is this check correct?
   First, most opponents automatically will bet with this type of board. And second, if you bet and are raised, you usually should call anyway. Thus, by checking, you get money in the pot when you have the best hand, but you save money those times when your opponent is very strong.

4. What if you have a hidden two pair or trips and are facing a three-straight or three-flush?
   Still check. Then you normally would call with two pair and check-raise with the trips (unless you are almost positive your opponent has a made hand.)

5. What if your two pair or trips include a pair on board?
   Be more inclined to bet.

Playing Big Cards Against a Medium Pair

1. Suppose on third street you have a hand like A♠K♦T♥ and a medium upcard such as an eight raises, meaning that you are against a likely medium pair. What should you do?

   Reraise if there is no more than one high card behind you and your hand is live. Otherwise fold.

2. Why?

   You would prefer to play heads-up.

3. What if you catch bad and your opponent catches a scare card on fourth street?

   Check and perhaps fold.

4. What if both you and your opponent catch bad?

   You usually should bet.

5. Why?

   This allows you to set up a steal on fifth street.

6. When is the time to attempt the steal on fifth street?

   When your opponent catches a second blank.

7. Example?

   Your opponent's board is something like ? ? 8♣2♦3♥. Bet no matter what you have.

Scare Card Strategy

1. What's an important consideration in determining whether to bet a weak hand?

   If you can get your opponent to fold on the next round if you catch a scare card.

2. Example?

   You raise with 10♣9♦J♠ and are called. You catch the A♠. You bet again and are called. You still should bet one more time if the next card is any spade, if it pairs your board, or if it is any other card such as an eight or nine that improves your hand.

3. Rephrase this idea.

   If your hand is worth a call or even almost worth a call if your opponent bets, it is better to bet yourself (even if there is no chance that your opponent will fold) if your bet may allow you to steal on the next round.

4. When might this occur?

   If you happen to catch a dangerous card, such as a pair card or suited card, that makes your opponent think that you are more of a favorite than you really are.

5. Although your bet will not always make your opponent more likely to fold on the next round, is it still sometimes worthwhile to bet?

   Yes.

6. Why?

   You make more money when your bet is called.

7. Example?

You have 2♣2♦8♠9♠, and you think your opponent has a straight draw or perhaps something like a pair of sixes. You still should bet, though he might fold on the next round even if you check on this round. The reason for betting is that many cards you can catch will make you more money when your opponent initially calls and then folds, or calls and then gets beat.

8. What are the cards which will help you to win the pot either eventually or on the next round?

Any deuce, eight, or nine, as well as any spade. Also possibly an ace, a seven, or a ten.

9. If you catch a scare card, should you always bet into a good aggressive player or a great player?

No.

10. Why?

Great players fear scary boards less than (reasonably) good players (but more than bad players).

11. Suppose on fourth street that you have a medium pair, a person in front of you bets, and a player behind you caught a scare card?

Usually throw your hand away.

12. Example?

You are second in a three-way pot and start with 8♥A♦8♠, and now catch a jack. A queen bets after catching a king, and the player behind you has caught a card that gives him two straight flush cards on board. Unless the pot is very large, throw your hand away immediately.

Buying the Free Card on Fourth Street

1. What's a standard play on fourth street that all good players make?

Against weak players, if someone bets on fourth street and you have any kind of scary board whatsoever, you should raise and then give yourself a free card on fifth street after he "checks to the raiser."

2. When is this play especially correct?

When your hand is likely to bet last on the following round.

3. What else should you keep in mind?

That this play works better if the fifth street cards that would make you first (to act) on that round would be good for you.

4. Example?

Your opponent has ? ? K♣5♠ and you have 8♥A♦8♠7♥. You should raise (as long as your opponent is a weak player), even if you are positive that you are against a pair of kings. Notice that the only cards you can catch to make you go first on the next round are cards that improve your hand.

5. After making this play, if your opponent checks to you on fifth street, do you always have to check if you don't improve?

No, an alternative strategy is to bet on fifth street and take a free card on sixth street when appropriate.

6. When would you not make this play?

Against a very good player you should often not make this play.

7. Why is that?

   You might be reraised or just called, but then bet into on the next round.

8. Example?

   You started with 4♣A♥4♥. Your opponent, whose door card is a face card, catches a non-threatening card on fourth street and bets. You can now raise, especially if your fourth-street card appears to go well with your door card and/or you now have a three-flush.

9. A more risky example?

   Your opponent has ? ? J♠3♣, and you have 8♥4♥8♣7♠. Notice that a raise in this spot has some drawbacks, since a queen, a king, or an ace will not help you very much, but may force you to bet first.

10. Should you still make the raise?

    Yes, you should still make this raise against weak opponents.

11. Why is that?

    Because they are so likely to check to you on the next round.

12. What if you now catch a high card and have to go first?

    You cannot get a free card unless your opponent is so timid that your raise on the previous round makes him afraid to bet even after you check.

13. What is the best counter strategy to the play we have been discussing?

    Call your opponent's raise on fourth street, and then go ahead and lead on fifth street when his card does not seem to help him and you think he was trying for a free card.

14. If raised again, do you give it up?
    You should still probably call. Remember, in seven-card stud you are almost never drawing that slim.

Buying the Free Card on Fifth Street

1. Is there a similar play to the one used on fourth street that can be used on fifth street?

   Yes.

2. Explain.

   If your opponent bets on fifth street and you have a hand that you plan to call with on both fifth and sixth streets, you might want to raise on fifth street. You would tend to do this when you are quite sure that your opponent will check to you on sixth street if you make this play.

3. When is this play especially worthwhile?

   If the card you catch on sixth street scared him out (incorrectly).

4. When is this play even better?

   If it is also true that the card that really does help you on sixth street does not scare him.

5. Example?

Suppose you have 7♥T♥T♠6♥4♥, and your opponent bets an apparent pair of jacks. You should raise, especially if you are almost certain that your raise will get your opponent to check on sixth street. (However, if he still will bet into you on sixth street, you don't really mind since your hand is almost as good as his.) Check it right back if you catch a blank. If you catch a heart, you bet, and your opponent should call (making you extra money), and if you pair the six or the four, your opponent likely will fold and you want him to. Also, bet again on sixth street if you catch an ace, a king, or a queen, and be prepared to bet on the river as a bluff.

6. Why will your opponent often fold when you pair?

He will be afraid that he is drawing dead.

An Expert Play

1. Suppose a good player with a strong upcard raises on third street and you call. On fourth street he catches "good" and you catch seemingly weak. He bets and you call. On fifth street he catches a strong card and you again catch what looks like a possible blank, and this time he checks. What should you usually do?

   Bet and expect to take the pot.

2. Example?

   Your opponent starts with an ace up, catches a king, and then catches a nine. You start with a jack up, catch a seven, and then are dealt a six. Bet on fifth street if your opponent checks after betting on the previous two rounds.

3. Why does this work?

   Your opponent has decided not to semi-bluff anymore and hopes he can represent a slowplay. Then, when you bet, your bet shows him that you must be strong. The idea is that when a good player checks what appears to be an obvious betting hand on fifth street, you often can steal the pot.

Throwing Fast Balls

1. What situation sometimes develops on fourth or fifth street?
You will be betting with what appears to be the best hand, but it has the potential to cost you a great deal of money.

2. Example?
You start with J♥4♦J♣. You raise and are called by a player whose upcard is lower than yours. On fourth street he catches an ace and you catch an inconsequential card.

3. Why does the ace create a problem for you?
It might have hit his hand.

4. What does a typical player do?
Bets on fourth street after their opponent checks, and again on fifth street.

5. What happens if they are against aces up?
They will be check-raised on fifth street, and will frequently continue with little chance.

6. Suppose you play your hand differently. When your opponent catches an ace on fourth street and checks, you check behind him. What's going to happen?
Your opponent will usually bet on fifth street. If he has aces up you will save a bet and a half. If he has a pair with an ace you have cost yourself a small fraction of a bet. And if he has nothing, you have extracted money from him.

7. On fourth street what if you catch a card that goes well with your door card?
You shouldn't check.

8. What is important to understand in stud?
   The better board should be in command.

9. What if your opponent wants to relinquish that right?
   It's often better to take a free card.

Playing in Loose Games

1. Against bad players is it detrimental to *mull* over your decisions?

Yes, it probably is.

2. Why?

When you sit there and think, you encourage bad players to play better against you.

3. What is it that you don't want to portray?

That you are capable of throwing away good hands for one more bet and that you look at every single decision critically.

4. When do you extract the most money from your opponents?

When you put them in a position to make big mistakes.

5. What should you do in a loose passive game where many people play on third street and then play poorly after that?

A. Play more hands, especially if you can get in for just the bring-in.

B. Often try to keep the early betting down to the size of the bring-in or just one full bet on third street.

6. With a hand that is *pretty* good but not great, what happens if you don't raise (and cost yourself a *little* bit of money at that point)?

You gain it back *plus* some because had you made the pot bigger there would be less opportunities for your opponents to make significant mistakes later on.

7. What if you're playing against extremely terrible opponents?

It's hard not to raise with pretty good hands even though you're costing yourself money on the later streets.

8. When there are many people in the pot, which hands go up in value?

The three-flushes, certain high three-card-straights, and even the ones that have gaps in them.

9. Example?

A hand like J♥9♥8♣ becomes fairly good because of the two-flush in addition to the straight cards if all of your cards are live.

10. If you have a poker hand that is good, but cannot improve, what is the mathematical paradox that you run into?

The more players drawing against you, the worse it is for you.

11. What does this mean as far as your strategy is concerned?

If your hand is simply good, but not great, it is important to try to thin the field down to one or two opponents.

12. Since early raises in loose games just cause you extra trouble with mediocre hands, what should your strategy be?

Put in as little money as possible early on with some of these questionable hands since you are often going to be folding on fourth or fifth street?

13. What is a second reason for this strategy?

Keeping the pot small early may allow you to thin the field out on the next round.

14. What about hands like 5♥A♦A♥ or J♣T♠J♠?

You should raise or reraise even in multiway pots as long as your hand is live.

15. Why?

    There is just too good a chance that you're going to make a hand that will be able to survive the onslaught of many players.

16. What is the trap that you don't want to get into?

    Calling with hands that won't make enough profitable situations.

17. Example?

    You throw away a hand like <u>9♥5♣</u>5♠, particularly if your hand is not live.

18. What hands can you play if you are in a loose, passive game where they usually call, but only occasionally raise?

    Any pair with a two-flush. A hand like <u>K♥Q♥</u>9♠ under the gun, and anything better.

19. Is it good if your big pair also contains a two-flush?

    It is a giant advantage.

20. Example?

    You hold <u>J♠8♠</u>J♥. If several players in front of you have just called, you should raise (unless your hand is dead) if you are in a game where the players are fairly weak.

21. For a raise with a hand like <u>Q♥7♣</u>Q♦ to be correct, what must you be able to accomplish?

    You must be able to limit the pot to only a small number of players.

22. What if your raise can't do this?

    Then you prefer to get in cheaply and make a decision on a later street as to how the hand should be played.

23. If a tough player to your right bets and there is a bad player to your left, and the situation is close between raising and calling, what should you do?

You should not raise.

Playing in Short-Handed Games

1. Should you change your strategy much when playing short-handed stud?

No. Unlike hold 'em, short-handed stud doesn't require that much change in your strategy.

2. Why?

There is less money in the pot in antes, and if you try to steal the antes too often your risk versus reward ratio changes.

3. What does this mean?

Those who try to steal too many antes in short-handed stud games are risking too much to win too little.

4. What if you stick to your normal, fairly tight game?

You really wouldn't be hurting yourself.

5. Why can short-handed poker be difficult for people who are trying to learn poker from books or who are used to full games?

It is simply that many ring game players never learn how to play mediocre hands well.

6. Do you meekly call with your poor hands against loose, aggressive players?

No.

7. What should you do?

Occasionally splash around, raising with hands that seem like they are barely worth calling.

8. Why do you do this?

To prevent your opponents from having a big edge from their semi-bluffs.

9. Example?

On fifth street you have 5♣5♦2♣9♦7♥, and your opponent has ? ? 2♥Q♣T♦. The right play may be to raise on fifth street.

10. What should you do if you are against someone who will raise only with a reasonable raising hand and who requires a legitimate calling hand to keep playing?

You should fire away.

11. When is this especially true?

If his board looks ragged.

Reading Hands

1. What is the most common way to read hands?

   Analyze the meaning of an opponent's check, bet, or raise and then look at the exposed cards and try to judge from them what his entire hand might be. You then combine the plays he has made *throughout the hand* with the exposed cards and come to a determination about his most likely hand.

2. Is it a mistake to put an opponent on a specific hand quite early and then stick to it?

   Yes.

3. On third street an opponent calls after you raise, then raises you on fourth street after catching a small suited card, but when you check to him on fifth street he also checks after catching a blank. What is a likely hand for him?

   A flush draw.

4. What if he catches a flush card on sixth street?

   You should not bet into him.

5. If he catches a blank on sixth street, what should you do?

   Bet, and then probably check on the river unless you think that he also has a pair and will call with it.

6. In this situation, what if you were on a flush draw and have missed it?

   You may now want to bet, since a reasonable chance exists that you can pick up the pot.

7. In practice, try to decide whether your opponent has what?

   A bad hand, a mediocre hand, a good hand, or a great hand.

8. If an opponent bets on the end, what type of hand is he unlikely to have?

    A mediocre hand.

9. What is a complimentary way to read hands?

    To work backwards.

10. If someone with a small card up cold calls a raise and a reraise by a king and an ace, catches nothing special, but is able to raise on sixth street, what is his probable starting hand?

    Since it does not seem possible that he would have called this far with something like a three-flush or a small pair, you have to suspect that he is rolled up.

11. When you can't actually put a person on a hand, but have reduced his possible holdings to a limited number, what do you use to determine the chances of his having certain hands rather than others?

    Mathematics.

12. Suppose an opponent, who is a tight player, starts with a medium card up and catches a third suited upcard on sixth street that is also an ace. Now he bets. You hold a hidden three-of-a-kind. If many of that suit already were exposed, especially on third street, what should you do?

    Raise. He probably has aces up.

13. What if the flush possibilities are live, and you think this is a possible hand for your opponent?

    You should just call and raise only if you make a full house or better on the river.

14. Suppose on third street you have A♣A♦4♠. You raise, and an opponent behind you reraises with an eight up. On fourth street, both you and your opponent pair your door cards, and he bets. What should you do?

> If you think your opponent is about equally likely to have a big pair in the hole (which is very unlikely to be aces) as another eight, you should at least call.

15. If you now catch an eight on fifth street and your opponent bets again, what is your play?

> Your play is to raise if you know this opponent would still bet if he had only two pair.

16. What is another factor in reading hands and deciding how to play your hand?

> The number of players in the pot.

17. How do players tend to play their hands in multiway pots?

> Much more straightforwardly.

18. When else is this true?

> If there are several players yet to act.

Psychology

1. What do we mean by the psychology of poker?
   Getting into your opponents' heads, analyzing how they think, figuring out what they think you think, and even determining what they think you think they think.

2. On third street you have the highest upcard and are in a late position, have little, and raise trying to steal the antes. You get reraised by a strong player who has the low card up and who knows that you automatically would try to steal in this position. What might be the correct play for you to make?
   To raise back and then to bet on fourth and fifth streets.

3. Would you make this play against a weak player?
   No.

4. When an opponent bets on the end in a situation where he is sure that you are going to call, is he bluffing?
   No.

5. Example?
   Suppose that you bet when all the cards are out, and a player raises you. It is rare to find an opponent who is capable of raising on the end as a bluff.

6. Is this true on fifth and sixth street?
   No. Tough players will raise on these streets if they hold a mediocre hand that has some potential to become a very strong hand.

7. When might your opponent be bluffing?
   When there appears to be a *good* chance that you will fold.

8. Example?

   No one bets on the fourth card and no one catches a scare card on fifth street. If one of your opponents now bets, and he is the type of player who would try to pick up the pot with nothing, it may be correct to call (or raise) with a relatively weak hand.

9. In deciding whether to bet, what else is equally important to consider?

   What your opponent thinks *you* have.

10. If your opponent suspects a strong hand, what should you do?

    Bluff more.

11. Example?

    You raise on fourth street with two suited cards, check when you catch a blank on fifth street, but bet when you catch a third suited card on sixth street. It is very hard for many of your opponents to call with only a pair. So bet your small pairs in this spot.

12. What if you know your opponent suspects that you are weak?

    You should not try to bluff, as you will get caught. But you should bet your fair hands for value.

13. Example?

    If both you and your opponent checked on sixth street, you frequently can bet one big pair on the end for value.

14. Should you ever intentionally make an "incorrect" play?

    Yes.

15. Why is that?

    You are trying to affect the thinking of your opponents for future hands.

16. Example?

    You occasionally can reraise on third street a late-position player with a high card up who may be on a steal when you hold something like a small three-flush (especially if your hand is live).

17. Who do these type of plays work well against?

    Players who are good enough to try to take advantage of their new-found knowledge, but who are not good enough to realize that you know this.

Questions and Answers

Afterthought

Again, these questions are not designed as a replacement for the material in the text. Their purpose is to help keep you sharp between complete readings of *Seven-Card Stud for Advanced Players*. We recommend that when you believe you have become a winning stud player that you reread the text material every other month and review the questions about once a week. Also, remember to cover the answers and to think through those questions that you have trouble with. In addition, attempt to relate the questions to recent hands that you have played, and try to determine which concepts were the correct ones to apply.

Another thing to keep in mind, as has been mentioned several times in this book, is that seven-card stud is an extremely complicated form of poker. This means that you should be a student of stud for life. Some forms of poker are much more simple, and you can master them in a relatively short period of time. One reason for this is that only a small number of situations can develop, and in time, you will know exactly what the correct strategy is for virtually every hand you play. Unfortunately, seven-card stud is not this way. It takes a long time to become an expert stud player. That is why continuous review of these questions (and the rest of the material in this book) is an absolute necessity.

Conclusion

As we've stated, the most important decision you will make in seven-card stud is whether or not to play your starting hand. In other words, most of the money is won or lost on the first round of play. It is certainly true that your decisions on the other streets can make a big difference in how much you win or lose, but your third-street decision is still the most important. This is why play on the first three cards received so much emphasis. Even so, those of you who make significant misplays on the later streets will be losers.

Perhaps the least known — and most controversial — advice given in this book has to do with playing weak hands when there has been no raise on third street. In fact, we expect that some readers will think we are playing too many hands in this situation and are only asking to get ourselves in trouble. Rest assured that this is not the case! All the authors know, not only from a theoretical point of view, but also from much practical experience, that many more hands than what the typical tight player plays can be played if there is not a raise on third street against the type of opponents found in most cardrooms.

We expect that this book will have a major impact not only on those of you who read and study it, but also on the games themselves. In general, there will begin to be more tough players around, meaning that some games will be tougher to beat. On the other hand, we also expect this text to be a significant contributor to the future growth of seven-card stud. Consequently, there will be many more games around, and the expert player will thus have more games from which to choose. We therefore expect that in the long run, this book will benefit those of you who make a commitment to studying the ideas it contains.

Appendix A: Match-Ups

When doing research for this book, we had the ability to do computer simulations. Some of these results are presented below with our comments.

Even though these types of results are useful in a game like seven-card stud, you should keep in mind that they are not poker. Specifically, they do not take into account how a hand is played, knowledge of your opponent, or the fact that the hand may not be played to the river. However, these results can give some important insights into whether and how a hand should be played. (Note: For each of these match-ups, the computer "dealt out" 100,000 hands. The result can be expected to be accurate to 0.5 percent.)

1. A♥A♦7♣ (66,604) versus Q♠Q♥7♦ (33,396)
Dead Cards: none
Comment: This result shows that it is rarely correct to play a smaller pair against a sure larger pair, unless you have an overcard kicker.

2. A♥A♦7♣ (63,893) versus Q♠Q♥7♠ (36,107)
Dead Cards: none
Comment: Having a two-flush does help a little bit but not enough to make this hand worth playing.

3. A♥A♦7♣ (63,159) versus Q♠Q♥7♦ (36,841)
Dead Cards: A♣
Comment: His dead ace is a little better than you having a two-flush, but again, the hand is not worth getting involved with if you are positive you are against the higher pair.

4. A♥A♠6♣ (61,441) versus 9♣9♦J♦ (38,559)
Dead Cards: none
Comment: This hand show the value of a straight flush kicker

5. A♥A♠6♣ (63,920) versus 9♣9♦J♥ (36,080)
Dead Cards: none
Comment: Just having a straight card for a kicker is not as strong.

6. A♥A♠6♣ (62,596) versus 5♣5♦3♦ (37,404)
Dead Cards: none
Comment: Another example of a straight flush kicker.

7. A♥A♦2♣ (66,704) versus 8♠8♣3♦ (33,296)
Dead Cards: none
Comment: This is another example of the strength of a big pair.

8. A♥A♦2♣ (69,846) versus 8♠8♣3♦A♣ (30,154)
Dead Cards: none
Comment: If you hold the larger pair, and your opponent catches your card, it helps rather than hurts, since it makes it harder for him to draw out.

9. K♠K♣8♥ (55,804) versus Q♥Q♦A♦ (44,196)
Dead Cards: none
Comment: An overcard kicker does make a difference. Also, the two-flush is of some help. Now you must play.

10. A♥A♦7♣ (68,439) versus J♠6♠2♠ (31,561)
Dead Cards: none
Comment: A three-flush against a bigger pair does not do very well in heads-up pots, unless it includes an overcard. (See #13 on page 301.)

11. A♥A♦7♥ (69,520) versus J♠6♠2♠ (30,480)
Dead Cards: none
Comment: Having a two-flush makes the hand with the big pair even stronger.

12. A♥A♦7♣ (72,676) versus J♠6♠2♠ (27,324)
Dead Cards: 5♠, Q♠
Comment: This shows the effect of having dead cards. The three-flush is now clearly unplayable heads-up.

13. Q♥Q♦7♣ (60,128) versus A♠9♠2♠ (39,872)
Dead Cards: none
Comment: Having an overcard with a three-flush makes a difference. It is definitely correct to take a card off, even in heads-up situations.

14. Q♥Q♦7♣ (63,618) versus A♠9♠2♠ (36,382)
Dead Cards: 5♠, 8♠
Comment: Again, this shows the effect of dead cards.

15. Q♥Q♦7♣ (57,955) versus T♠9♠7♠ (42,045)
Dead Cards: None
Comment: This match-up clearly shows that a three-card-straight flush is clearly playable against an overpair.

16. Q♥Q♦7♣ (71,232) versus 8♠9♥10♣ (28,768)
Dead Cards: none
Comment: Notice that the three-straight is not that live since two queens and a seven are in the other hand. The three-straight therefore should be thrown away.

17. Q♥Q♦7♣ (68,901) versus 4♠5♥6♣ (31,099)
Dead Cards: none
Comment: This three-straight is more live than the previous one and does better. It is still probably wrong however to take a card off since it has no overcards.

18. Q♥Q♦7♣ (71,999) versus 4♠5♥6♣ (28,001)
Dead Cards: 3♣, 3♠
Comment: Again, this illustrates the effect of dead cards.

19. J♣8♣6♣3♣ (51,617) versus A♥A♦9♣2♠ (48,383)
Dead Cards: none
Comment: On fourth street, a four-flush is usually a slight favorite over a big pair.

20. J♣8♣6♣3♣ (57,230) versus 9♥9♦7♣3♠ (42,770)
Dead Cards: none
Comment: When the four-flush includes an overcard, it is an even bigger favorite. A raise is thus frequently in order.

21. A♣Q♣9♣4♣ (62,097) versus 10♥10♦9♠7♥ (37,903)
Dead Cards: none
Comment: Two overcards make things even better.

22. J♦J♣7♣5♣4♣ (59,888) vs A♥A♦8♠6♠3♥ (40,112)
Dead Cards: none
Comment: On fifth street, a pair and a four-flush is a significant favorite against a bigger pair. Again this usually means raise.

23. A♥K♦Q♣ (38,642) versus 9♠9♥T♦ (61,358)
Dead Cards: none
Comment: Three overcards against a pair is a marginal hand (especially with only one straight possibility). This result may surprise many readers.

24. A♥K♦Q♥ (40,199) versus 9♠9♥T♦ (59,801)
Dead Cards: none
Comment: A two-flush helps the three high cards a little.

25. A♥K♦Q♣ (41,728) versus 9♠9♥3♦ (58,272)
Dead Cards: none
Comment: The pair now does slightly poorer since it does not have a two-straight.

26. 6♥7♦8♥ (51,329) versus J♠J♥3♦ (48,671)
Dead Cards: J♦, J♣, 3♠, 3♥, 3♣
Comment: Here's what happens when your hand is completely dead. It's an underdog to a small three-card straight. That's why we tell you to dump hands such as this.

27. 8♥9♦T♣ (45,940) versus 7♠7♥2♦ (54,060)
Dead Cards: none
Comment: The three-straight (with the three overcards) would have done even better had the pair of sevens not been in the opposing hand. Still, the three-straight is easily worth playing.

28. J♥J♦9♣3♠2♥ (65,899) versus 6♦6♣10♠5♥4♦ (34,101)
Dead Cards: none
Comment: A small pair with no overcards is a big dog to a larger pair on fifth street. Thus it should be folded, especially since it already may be against two pair.

29. J♥J♦9♣3♠2♥ (61,308) versus 6♦6♣A♠5♥4♦ (38,692)
Dead Cards: none
Comment: The ace does make the hand playable.

30. J♥J♦9♥3♥2♥ (74,911) versus 6♦6♣A♠5♥4♦ (25,089)
Dead Cards: none
Comment: The ace does not help enough if you are up against a four-flush as well as the big pair.

31. J♥J♦9♣3♠2♥ (60,508) versus 6♦6♣A♠K♥4♦ (39,492)
Dead Cards: none
Comment: The second overcard helps a little more.

32. J♥J♦9♣3♠2♥ (55,728) vs 6♦6♣A♠K♥Q♦ (44,272)
Dead Cards: none
Comment: Now this hand has not only three overcards but straight potential as well.

33. J♥J♦9♣3♠2♥ (62,562) versus 6♦6♣10♦5♥4♦ (37,438)
Dead Cards: none
Comment: Having a three-flush and a three-straight with the small pair does make a difference.

34. J♥J♦9♣3♠2♥ (64,897) versus 6♦6♣10♦9♥4♦ (35,103)
Dead Cards: none
Comment: Having only a three-flush with the small pair means that your decision to continue on will be a close one.

35. Q♥Q♦A♦ (62,699) versus K♠6♠4♠ (37,301)
Dead Cards: none
Comment: The overcard to the pair helps the three-flush.

36. J♥J♦J♣ (85,425) versus A♠A♥2♦ (14,575)
Dead Cards: none
Comment: Rolled up trips is a very strong starting hand.

37. J♥J♦J♣ (89,607) versus A♥A♦2♣J♠ (10,493)
Dead Cards: none
Comment: When you have trips, if your opponent catches your card, it helps more than it hurts if he was drawing to one or two pair.

38. J♥J♦J♣ (72,399) versus 2♥2♦2♣ (27,601)
Dead Cards: none
Comment: Having the higher rolled up hand is a large advantage.

39. 2♥2♦2♣8♠ (75,880) versus A♥A♦K♣K♠ (24,120)
Dead Cards: none
Comment: Even a hand with two big pairs does not fare well against a set.

40. J♥J♦4♣4♠ (55,182) versus A♥A♦2♣6♠ (44,818)
Dead Cards: none
Comment: A big pair does okay against two smaller pair. Clearly you must "chase" to the river.

41. A♥A♦2♣6♠ (59,314) versus J♥J♦6♥9♥ (40,686)
Dead Cards: none
Comment: Having a pair with a three-flush is enough to continue playing on fourth street against a larger pair.

42. J♥J♦4♣4♠ (77,003) versus 3♥3♦2♣2♠ (22,997)
Dead Cards: none
Comment: Small two pair does not fare well against a larger two pair and should be thrown away.

43. 3♥3♦2♣2♠ (51,515) versus J♥J♦6♥9♥ (48,485)
Dead Cards: none
Comment: A small two pair versus a larger pair with a three-flush is only a small favorite.

44. K♣K♥3♠ (41,511) (versus) Q♦Q♠2♣ (26,591) versus J♥A♣J♠ (31,898)
Dead Cards: none
Comment: The small pair with the big overcard kicker is playable in this three way confrontation. The pair in the middle has the worst of it.

45. K♣K♥3♠ (44,834) (versus) Q♦Q♠2♣ (28,127) versus J♥A♣J♠ (27,039)
Dead Cards: J♦
Comment: The missing jack makes the hand probably not worth playing.

46. Q♣Q♠2♦ (40,487) (versus) T♥T♦4♠ (27,507) versus 5♥K♦5♠ (32,006)
Dead Cards: None
Comment: Another example of how the overcard kicker makes the small pair playable against two larger pairs.

47. Q♣Q♦6♥ (26,241) (versus) Q♠Q♥7♣ (27,862) versus 4♦4♠A♥ (45,897)
Dead Cards: None
Comment: A small pair with a large overcard kicker is a big money favorite against two players who each hold a large pair of the same rank.

48. Q♣Q♦2♥ (30,916) (versus) Q♠Q♥3♣ (33,642) versus 9♥8♠7♦ (35,442)
Dead Cards: None
Comment: Even a three-straight with no overcards is a favorite against two of the same pair.

Appendix B: Glossary

Action: The betting in a particular hand or game. A game with a lot of action is a game with a lot of betting. The player who starts the action is the player who makes the first bet.

Active player: A player still in the pot.

All-in: Having all one's money in the pot.

Ante: A bet required from all players before the start of a hand.

Back door: Three cards to a flush or a straight, after five cards have been dealt. In general, the term is used for a hand made on the end, which a player was not originally trying to make.

Bad beat: Having a hand that is a big favorite defeated as the result of a lucky draw, especially when the person drawing was playing incorrectly by being in the pot in the first place.

Bad game: A game in which your opponents are too good for you to expect to win much.

Bankroll: The amount of money you have available to wager.

Best of it: A situation in which a wager can be expected to be profitable in the long run.

Bet: To put money in the pot before anyone else on any given round.

Bettor: The person who first puts money in the pot on any given round.

Bet for value: To bet in order to be called by a lesser hand. You are betting to make money, not to make your opponents fold.

Blank: A card that is not of any value to a player's hand.

Bluff: A bet or raise with a hand you do not think is the best hand.

Board: The cards that are face up in a player's hand.

Bring-in: The forced bet that the lowest card showing must make.

Bring it in: To start the betting on the first round.

Busted hand: A hand that does not develop into anything of value.

Buy in: The minimum amount of money required to sit down in a particular game.

Call: To put in the pot an amount of money equal to an opponent's bet or raise.

Call a raise cold: To call a double bet — that is, a bet and a raise.

Caller: A person who calls a bet or raise.

Card room: The area in a casino where poker (and sometimes panguingue) is played.

Chase: To continue in a hand trying to outdraw an opponent's hand you are quite sure is better than yours.

Check: To decline to bet when it is your turn.

Check-raise: To check and then raise after an opponent bets.

Chip: A round token in various denominations representing money. Among many professional gamblers it is also called a "check."

Cinch: The best possible hand, given the cards on board, when all the cards are out.

Come hand: A hand that has not yet been made, with more cards still to be dealt. Thus, a four-card flush would be a come hand.

Crying call: A call with a hand you think has a small chance of winning.

Cut the pot: To take a percentage from each pot as the profits for the person or the casino running the game.

Dead hand: A hand a player may not continue to play because of an irregularity.

Dead money: Money put in the pot by players who have already folded their hands.

Door card: The first exposed card in a player's hand.

Drawing dead: Drawing to try to make a hand that cannot possibly win because an opponent already holds a bigger hand. A player drawing to make a flush when an opponent already has a full house is drawing dead.

Draw out: To improve your hand so that it beats an opponent who had a better hand than yours prior to your draw.

Early position: A position on a round of betting in which you must act before most of the other players.

Edge: An advantage over an opponent.

Effective odds: The ratio of the total amount of money you expect to win if you make your hand to the total amount of bets you will have to call to continue from the present round of betting to the end of the hand.

Equity: The value of a particular hand or combination of cards.

Expectation: The average profit (or loss) of any bet over the long run.

Family pot: A pot in which most of the players at the table are involved.

Favorite: In poker, before all the cards are out, a hand that has the best chance of winning.

Fifth street: The fifth card to be dealt to each player.

Fill: To draw a card that makes a hand. For example, to fill a flush is to draw a fifth card of that suit.

Fill up: To make a full house.

Flat call: To call a bet without raising.

Flush: Five cards of the same suit.

Fold: To drop out of a pot rather than call a bet or raise.

Forced bet: A required bet to start the action on the first round of a poker hand. For example, usually the low card on board must make a forced bet.

Four-flush: Four cards to a flush.

Four-of-a-kind: Four cards of the same rank. Four jacks is four-of-a-kind.

Fourth street: The fourth card dealt to each player.

Free card: A card that a player gets without having to call a bet.

Full house: Three cards of one rank and two of another. A♣A♥A♦9♠9♥ is a full house.

Giving a hand away: Playing your hand in such a way that your opponents should know what you have.

Good game: A game in which there are enough players worse than you, for you to be a substantial favorite.

Gut shot: A draw to an inside straight.

Heads-up: Playing against a single opponent.

Hole: The concealed cards.

Hourly rate: The amount of money a player expects to win per hour on average.

Implied odds: The ratio of the total amount of money you expect to win if you make your hand to the bet you must now call to continue in the hand.

Inside straight: A straight which can be made only with a card of one rank, usually somewhere in the middle of the straight. When you hold ten-nine-seven-six, only an eight will give you a straight. Thus, you are drawing to an inside straight, or you have an inside-straight draw. Ace-king-queen-jack is also an inside straight draw.

Kicker: A side card, usually a high one. Someone holding A♦9♦9♥ has a pair of nines with an ace *kicker*.

Late position: A position on a round of betting in which you act after most of the other players have acted.

Legitimate hand: A hand with value; a hand that is not a bluffing hand.

Limit: The amount a player may bet or raise on any round of betting.

Limit poker: A poker game where the minimum and maximum amounts a player may bet or raise on any given round of betting are fixed.

Limp in: To call a bet rather than raise. (This usually applies only to the first round of betting.)

Live card: In stud games a card that has not yet been seen and is therefore presumed likely to be still in play.

Live one: A loose, weak player with a lot of money to lose.

Lock: A cinch hand. A hand that cannot lose.

Long shot: A hand that has little chance of being made.

Loose: Playing more hands than the norm.

Loose game: A game with lots of players in most pots.

Mathematical expectation: The mathematical calculation of what a bet can be expected to win or lose on average.

Middle position: A position on a round of betting somewhere in the middle. In an eight-handed game, the fourth, fifth, and sixth players to act would be said to be in middle position.

Muck: To discard a hand.

Multiway pot: A pot in which more than two players are involved.

Negative expectation: The amount a wager may be expected to lose on average. A play with negative expectation is a play that will lose money over the long run.

Nuts: The best possible hand at any given point in a pot.

Odds: The chances, expressed mathematically, that an event will occur. Also, in the term *pot odds,* the ratio of the size of the pot to the amount of the bet you must call to continue.

Off-suit: Not of the same suit.

On the come: Playing a hand that has not yet been made. For instance, if you bet with four cards to a flush, you are betting on the come.

On tilt: Playing much worse than usual because, for one reason or another, you have become emotionally upset.

Open-ended straight: Four cards to a straight, which can be made with cards of two different ranks. Thus, nine-eight-seven-six is an open-ended straight, which can be made with either a ten or a five. Theoretically, jack-nine-eight-seven-five is also open-ended in that either a ten or a six will make the hand.

Open pair: An exposed pair.

Outs: Cards which will improve your hand. Also, ways of improving your hand. The term is used particularly in reference to a hand that needs to improve to become the best hand.

Overcall: A call of a bet after another player has already called.

Overcard: A card higher than any card your opponent has showing.

Pair: Two cards of the same rank. Two eights is a *pair.*

Pass: To check. Also, to fold.

Pay off: To call a bet or raise when you don't think you have the best hand.

Pay station: A player who calls bets and raises much more than is correct. He's also referred to as a *calling station.* This type is great to be against when you have a legitimate hand, but he's just about impossible to bluff out of a pot.

Pocket: Another term for hole. Thus, two aces in the pocket means two aces in the hole.

Position: The spot in the sequence of betting in which a player is located. A player in first position would be the first person to act; a player in last position would be the last person to act.

Positive expectation: The amount a wager may be expected to win on average. A play with positive expectation is a play that will win money over the long run.

Pot: The total amount of money wagered at any point in a hand. A hand itself is also referred to as a pot. Thus, three people in the pot means there are three active players still playing the hand.

Pot odds: The ratio of the amount of money in the pot to the bet you must call to continue in the hand.

Put someone on a hand: To determine as best you can the hand (or hands) an opponent is most likely to have.

Pure nuts: The best possible hand. The pure nuts is much more common in flop games than it is in stud games.

Rag: *See* Blank.

Raise: To bet an additional amount after someone else has bet.

Raiser: A player who raises.

Rake: An amount retained by a casino from each pot, usually no more than $3.

Represent: To make your opponents believe you have a particular hand. Thus, if you raise with an ace showing, you are representing a pair of aces. You may or may not in fact have a pair of aces.

Reraise: To raise after an opponent has raised.

Reverse implied odds: The ratio of the amount of money now in the pot to the amount of money you will have to call to continue from the present round to the end of the hand.

River: The seventh and last card, dealt face down.

Rolled up: Three-of-a-kind on the first three cards.

Round of betting: A sequence of betting after one or more cards have been dealt. A round of betting continues until each active player has either folded or called.

Royal flush: An ace-high straight flush. A♠K♠Q♠J♠10♠ is a royal flush.

Rush: Several winning hands in a short period of time.

Sandbag: To play weakly with a strong hand. To check-raise or slowplay with the probable best hand.

Scare card: An upcard that looks as though it might have made a strong hand.

Score: A big win.

Seat charge: In public card rooms, an hourly fee for playing poker.

Semi-bluff: To bet with a hand which you do not think is the best hand but which has a reasonable chance of improving to the best hand.

Set: Three-of-a-kind.

Seventh street: The seventh card dealt to each player.

Short-stacked: Playing in a game with a relatively small number of chips remaining.

Showdown: The turning up of all active players' cards at the end of the final round of betting to see who has the best hand.

Side pot: A second pot for the other active players when one player is all-in.

Sixth street: The sixth card dealt to each player.

Slowplay: To check or just call an opponent's bet with a big hand in order to win more money on later rounds of betting.

Starting requirement: The minimum initial hand a player considers he needs to continue in a pot.

Start the action: To make the first bet in a particular hand.

Steal: To cause your opponents to fold when you probably do not have the best hand. The term is used especially in reference to stealing the antes — that is, raising on the first round of betting so that everyone remaining in the pot folds.

Steal the antes: *See* above.

Steam: To play badly because you are emotionally upset — especially to play considerably more pots than you normally would when your hands do not justify it.

Straight: Five cards of mixed suits in sequence. 10♦9♣8♥7♦6♥ is a straight.

Straight flush: Five cards of the same suit in sequence. 10♥9♥8♥7♥6♥ is a straight flush.

Structure: The limits set upon the ante, forced bets, and subsequent bets and raises in any given game.

Stuck: Losing money, especially a substantial amount of money, in a given session or over a period of time. We might say, "Sammy is stuck $1,500 in the game." That is, Sammy has lost $1,500.

Sucker: A player who can be expected to lose money, especially one who is not as good as he thinks.

Suited: Two or more cards of the same suit.

Tell: A mannerism a player has that may give away his hand.

Three-of-a-kind: Three cards of the same rank. 7♠7♦7♥ is *three-of-a-kind.*

Third Street: The third card dealt to each player.

Three-flush: Three cards of the same suit.

Tight: Playing fewer hands than the norm.

Tight game: A game with a small number of players in most pots.

Trips: Three-of-a-kind.

Two-flush: Two cards of the same suit.

Underdog: A hand that does not have the best chance of winning.

Under the gun: The first person to act on the first round of betting is under the gun. On later betting rounds, the player to the immediate left of the bettor is said to be under the gun.

Up: Expressions like aces up, kings up, and sixes up mean two pair with two aces, two kings, or two sixes as the highest of the two pair. Unless an opponent has a top pair of the same rank, the rank of the second pair is of no importance.

Upcard: A card that is dealt face up.

Value: What a hand is worth in terms of its chances of being the best hand.

Wired pair: A pair in the hole.

World Series of Poker: An annual series of poker tournaments with buy-ins ranging up to $10,000, which is held each spring at the Horseshoe Casino in Las Vegas. The competition is generally recognized as the premier competition among the best poker players in the world.

Worst of it: A situation in which a wager will be unprofitable in the long run.

Index